MARCO ⊕ POLO
EASTERN USA

with Local Tips
The author's special recommendations are highlighted in yellow throughout this guide

D0907428

There are five symbols to help you find your way around this guide:

★

Marco Polo's top recommendations – the best in each category

\\!/

sites with a scenic view

◉

where the local people meet

⚲

where young people get together

(100/A1)
pages and coordinates for the road atlas

MARCO ⊕ POLO

Travel guides and language guides in this series:

Algarve • Amsterdam • Australia • Berlin • Brittany • California
Channel Islands • Costa Brava/Barcelona • Costa del Sol/Granada
Côte d'Azur • Crete • Cuba • Cyprus • Eastern USA • Florence • Florida
Gran Canaria • Greek Islands/Aegean • Ibiza • Ireland • Istanbul • Lanzarote
London • Mallorca • Malta • New York • New Zealand • Normandy • Paris
Prague • Rhodes • Rome • Scotland • South Africa • Southwestern USA
Tenerife • Turkish Coast • Tuscany • Venice • Western Canada

French • German • Italian • Spanish

*Marco Polo would be very interested to hear your
comments and suggestions. Please write to:*

North America:
Marco Polo North America
70 Bloor Street East
Oshawa, Ontario, Canada
(B) 905-436-2525

United Kingdom:
World Leisure Marketing Ltd
Marco Polo Guides
Newmarket Drive
Derby DE24 8NW

*Our authors have done their research very carefully, but should any errors or omissions
have occurred, the publisher cannot be held responsible for any injury, damage
or inconvenience suffered due to incorrect information in this guide*

Cover photograph: White House in Washington (Fotex: Stock Imagery)
*Photos: Lade: BAV (54, 68), Bramaz (11); Layda (4, 46, 60); Mauritius: Hubatka (99),
Messerschmidt (64), Noble (72), Schmied (79), Superstock (22), Thonig (36), Torino (86),
Vidler (5 pm, 74); Schapowalow: China Photo (49, 80), Fahn (26), Heaton (14), Lensch (31),
Messerschmidt (8); Schuster: Bull (40), Schmied (21), Steinkamp (94); Teuschl (45);
Transglobe: Baier (28), Granitsas (57, 63), Haas (53), Harris (6), Thomas (20)*

1st edition 1999
© Mairs Geographischer Verlag, Ostfildern, Germany
Author: Michael Schwelien and Karl Teuschl
Translation: Mellissa Knabe
English edition 1999: Gaia Text
Editorial director: Ferdinand Ranft
Chief editor: Marion Zorn
Cartography Road Atlas: © SGA Ltd. (MapArt), Canada
Design and layout: Thienhaus/Wippermann
Printed in Germany

CONTENTS

Discover the Eastern US!

Compare what you envisioned with what you actually find

*T*he East Coast girls are really hip/I dig the styles they wear – just a line from one of the hits by the Beach Boys. However, the refrain which follows the praise the band sings for the fashionable style of the East Coast girls is full of yearning for something completely different: *I wish they all could be California girls.*

An old hit about the same old story. What's better? The East or the West Coast? It's a song about the good-natured regional competition within the United States. But the differences between East and West are often more prevalent in the minds of the people than in reality.

In the past, the differentiation was understandable. Well into the 19th century the West truly was wild and simultaneously full of promise. *'Go west, young man!'* Young people were called to head westward in search of happiness. Even today, the stereotype remains: The East is viewed as a bastion of established

New England is known for its neoclassical architecture, such as the State House in Boston

wealth, power, culture and tradition. The West emanates a fast-paced, modern and dynamic flair. A cliché: East Coast = old-fashioned, West Coast = progressive.

This myth continues to have an influence on the American political scene as well. When Ronald Reagan was elected president, he was certainly an endearing elderly man, but hardly a renewer. Yet it was said that a 'revolution' was starting in California which would change the entire country.

Reagan's successor, George Bush, who was born and raised in the oldest part of the country, New England, stressed that he was from Texas in order to assume the image of the modern man.

Of course, it's impossible to deny the fact that the New World was settled all along the East Coast by Europeans, and any structures that date back further than 100 years are to be found primarily in the East.

Yet, with regard to intellectual, economical and cultural aspects, there is no major difference between the two coasts. America has remained a giant merry-go-round. It seems as if Americans are constantly migrating from one place to another: from North to South whilst others move from East to West, and back again. Thanks to this mobility, the country is constantly evolving and revealing new sides. If you have stayed in any one place for a while and you think you have gained a certain impression of that one area, then you'll often find you have to revise that impression because changes occur overnight.

Let's take a look at the Massachusetts state capital. Boston is the honourable grandmother of American cities. It wasn't long ago that Boston was regarded as a dull and dusty old place. Almost overnight, a computer

Replica of the Mayflower, *which brought the first settlers to the New World*

and a genetic engineering industry that is more innovative than Silicon Valley developed in the Boston area. However, then a number of bankruptcies oc-

curred among the widespread risk investments, and Boston hit rock bottom again, only to be revived once more during the general economic boom.

New York is another perfect example: How often the epitomy of a metropolis, has this city of cities, been pronounced dead? The city is bankrupt, overcome by crime and deterioration – that might sound up-to-date, but in reality it's totally outdated. New York has now become the model city in fighting crime across the world. Plus the fact that New York has always been a centre for the arts and the meeting place for the elite.

Or Atlanta. Who wouldn't think of Scarlett O'Hara and those classic scenes in that all-time favoured movie *Gone with the Wind*? Yet it would be hopeless to start searching for the plantation mansions with their huge Greek columns in this city, which stands for the former Deep South. It's hopeless to try and find sleepy Peachtree Street. Atlanta is something totally different, an urban air conditioner, the most progressive city planning experiment in the entire world with the goal of placing the entire downtown area under one roof. Atlanta's downtown area is built to allow all activity to take place in a gigantic, covered mall full of hotels, shopping malls and office buildings. The core is in the centre of the city of Atlanta, thus remaining hidden from view.

And Florida, the haven for the retired? Within the last decade, a transformation has taken place in Florida, one that would be unlikely elsewhere, even in the course of generations. Today, college and high school students dance the night away where the retired once enjoyed the evening sun while rocking in their lawn chairs.

The Art Deco quarter of Miami Beach, which was built in the '20s and '30s and had so decayed by the '60s and '70s that it faced demolition due to the fact that some of the older buildings had become dangerous, has once more become a polished jewel. Miami is now so popular that nearly every fashion magazine in the world considers it to be a necessary backdrop for photographing the newest designer collections. It seems as fashion and Miami Beach now seem to be joined inseparably.

In the meantime, states such as Kentucky and Tennessee have surprisingly developed into industrial areas with a number of automobile assembly lines that were previously exclusively located in the Michigan factories of Detroit and Flint. America's East Coast is certainly not the honourable yet outdated half of the country. And America is not only found in California, as was once suggested in the title of a book about this West Coast state.

The complex soul of the country can be explored along the Atlantic just as much as along the Pacific coast. What divides the country today is something other than geography. It is the socio-economic gap between rich and poor that is becoming apparent throughout the United States. The world's poor and suffering have historically turned their eyes toward America, where the Consitution acknowledges their right to life, liberty and the pursuit of happiness. During the past 100 years, this echo has resounded from the New World to the people of the Old World. That's what 'Lady Liberty', one of the most famous landmarks in the world, stands for.

The *Statue of Liberty*, which stands in New York's harbour, was unveiled in 1886 as 'Liberty Enlightening the World', a gift from France to the United States. The sculptor Frédéric-Auguste Bartholdi and the engineer Gustave Eiffel, who also built the famous Eiffel Tower in Paris, designed the Statue of Liberty. A great amount of water has flowed down the Hudson River ever since Lady Liberty, comprised of 444,000 pounds (222 tonnes) of copper plates over a steel frame, first illuminated the world.

Even though she received an extensive and costly facelift prior to the Centennial celebration of her unveiling in 1986, a little rust has reappeared, and she's not the only one. Another monument located on New York's Upper West Side is the replica of the antique mausoleum of Halicarnassus. This monument, which marks the grave of Civil War General and President Ulysses S. Grant, symbolizes the societal side of the passing of history. That is, it's actually the park where the marble and granite mausoleum of the commander of the union army is located, which stands for the passing of history.

America is as much a country of the poor and suffering as it is of the rich and superwealthy. If Charles Dickens were to rewrite his novel about the proximity of glory and horror, *A Tale of Two Cities*, then he would have to exchange the setting of the novel from Paris during the time of the revolution to modern New York or to one of the other metropolitan areas of this country whose countless tourists are greeted by the following words on the customs declaration slip: *'Welcome to the United States of America!'*

The cities of the East Coast form a singular, gigantic megalopolis that extends from Boston to Washington, D.C. Beyond the borders of this huge urban area, you'll find flat countryside that has a low population density in some areas – at least flat in relation to the ridges of the Appalachian mountains that rise just beyond the coast, running nearly parallel to the Atlantic. This low mountain range is high enough to make the Black

Forest in Germany or the Vosges Mountains in France look like anthills. The Appalachians run from the St. Lawrence Seaway in the north to the Gulf of Mexico in the south, 2,600 km (1,625 miles) long and up to 600 km (375 miles) wide. The highest peaks have an altitude of between 1,500 and 2,000 m (4,875-6,500 ft).

Autumn, when the leaves start changing colour, is a breathtakingly beautiful season here. When the sun shines, the area enjoys beautiful Indian summer days. Travelling to see the autumn *foliage* has become a favourite excursion for many Americans. The weather report announces where the line wandering between the cooler North and the warmer South currently is, indicating where to find green leaves that have turned to a medly of lemon yellow, gold, bright orange and burgundy red.

Soon after crossing the mountains, that is, about a day's drive by car, you'll arrive at the Great Lakes, inland freshwater highways used by ocean vessels. The cities of Cleveland, Detroit and Chicago are located along the Great Lakes. All these cities are symbolic of the classical industrial areas. Americans often speak of the Rust Bowl, meaning the entire Northeast, which once thrived on the coal and steel industries, and on trade and technology, and where the assembly line was invented (Ford) and the labour unions battled fiercely the Labor Day holiday (the first Monday in September). The giants of the Industrial Age have

The Statue of Liberty in New York

had to seek new ways to keep up with the changing needs of companies.

Many modern companies prefer the so-called Sunshine Economy, the economic system of the South which not only lowers overhead by saving heating costs, but also relieves employers of such factors as labour unions, employment protection agencies and health insurance.

The huge industries of the North have learned to be more cost-effective in recent years and are once more making profits on the world's markets. As it's called in economic jargon, more modern companies have gained locational independence. The booming computer, aeronautics and service industries did not ignore the North, so that even a city like Pittsburgh, the former steel town, was revived. The result of changing economic times is a duality that is evident everywhere. One sees flashy modernity and unbounded vitality juxtaposed with deteriorated downtown and huge deserted factory buildings, their windows cracked and smashed. The industrial wasteland reflects the pioneering spirit that reigns in the eastern USA. If someone feels there's no future for him in one area, he moves on to the next.

Even in Detroit, which was hit especially hard by the industrial transformation, the stereotype of wasteland cannot be taken too literally. Once more: two cities in one – Detroit also has a second, modern face. The Renaissance Center, a downtown skyscraper complex which was erected with subsidies during the era of President Jimmy Carter, has been joined by other structures.

And now for New York, 'the city that doesn't sleep.' Countless songs have been written extolling the virtues of the great metropolis. Frank Sinatra's hit evokes the extraordinary zest for life this dynamic city possesses and expresses the fascination it holds for both those who live there and those who dream of going there. For many people it is the capital city of the American Dream.

The only way to really understand this thriving city, and the reason for its international influence, is to experience it first hand – 'to wake up in the city that doesn't sleep' to the sound of honking horns, the constant hum of traffic and wailing sirens, and to venture out into the thick of New York street life.

No other city in the world can profess to being more ruthless than New York. Yet, people can become attached to it. Visitors are either enthralled by it or put off by it, but those who leave the city with fond memories and a desire to return far outnumber those who don't.

New York is a modern city in a state of constant flux and regeneration, a city that lives in the present, thriving from the energy of its people, the dynamics of money, the pressure of immense competition and the pursuit of success.

New York is the undisputed capital of trade and commerce: it is hectic, loud, challenging, merciless and powerful. Manhattan is not an industrial centre, but a control centre. It is the place where affairs are managed and buttons pressed. As the media capital of the USA, New York is the centre of information and popular culture. All the major publishing houses, record companies and music publishers have their head offices in the city and operate from here with their sights set firmly on the world markets.

Between the juxtaposition of wealth and poverty, great and small, old and new, there is astonishing diversity. Every race, nation and creed can be found in New York. In the words of Quentin Crisp, 'when you are in this city, you feel you are at the heart of the world'. The majority who emigrated here have made their homes here for political or economic reasons. Driven by hope for a better future and not willing to accept the situations they were in or the hardships they had to endure, they brought their cultures and traditions with them.

Even today, the population of New York is in constant flux. During the last century, Europeans from Ireland, Germany, Austria and Russia emigrated to America, thus altering the traditionally English-speaking environment. At the beginning of this century, immigrants from Italy and Poland arrived in droves. When the Nazis came to power in Germany, and during World War II, New York became a safe haven for Jews fleeing persecution.

A multifaceted unity has thus emerged. New York City has a unique racial mix. With millions of Spanish-speaking immigrants from Central and South America, with hundreds of thousands of Chinese, Koreans and Vietnamese and with the influx of many black Americans from the American South, the city, although beginning to lose its integrative abilities, is still a simmering melting pot.

Especially in the northeast is the American affinity for European culture evident. American opera enthusiasts flock to see such stars as Luciano Pavarotti and Placido Domingo, who appear at the New York City Metropolitan Opera.

Many aspects of everyday life in the United States are already familiar to most foreign visitors. Television series and T-shirts, Broadway shoes and Coca-Cola, Nike sports shoes and Ray-Ban sunglasses: these symbols of the American way of life are well known around the world.

The United States is a country of open and unabashed patriotism. Miniatures of the nation's red, white and blue flag, referred to by Americans as 'Old Glory', flutter from the windows of neat little homes in small-town America, and school children across the nation often begin their school day by chanting the words: *I pledge allegiance to the flag of the United States of America.*

Somewhere between the two extremes of small towns and big metropolises, you'll find the fictitious city of Middletown, America, a symbol of ideal American life: neat homes with well-tended lawns, barbecues, baseball fields and churches. You'll encounter the real version often enough when travelling through the eastern part of the

United States, making your trip a journey of revelations.

All along the highways leading into medium-sized towns, you'll find strips of car dealerships. Their sales areas are marked by strings of brightly-coloured flags and chains of lights.

Sometimes, the most remarkable monuments across America are those that are not readily apparent, namely the structures of Middletown America: simple wooden houses, a villa from the town's founding period, a movie theatre from the '20s, a neoclassical bank or a postmodern office building – either beautifully preserved or recently erected.

The eastern part of America comprises far less than half of the country. Its major cities are best described with one word: contrast.

Take the nation's capital, for example. Washington, D.C. is the nation's seat of power, yet at times, it has the rhythm of a small southern town. Central areas are meticulously groomed and laid out, with graceful neoclassical buildings. But these areas often border on neglected slums. These, in turn, give way to extremely wealthy suburbs and the hills of Virginia where horses graze in lush pastures enclosed by immaculate white fences. That's where the Old South, the former Confederacy, begins.

You'll discover this as well: outside the large cities, characteristics of the South have survived. The countryside seems sluggish in the burning heat of the long southern summer. The air is humid, the language slow with the *Southern drawl* – no one puts a strain on his voice here. It only takes about two hours to drive from the centre of power, where important decisions are made financially and politically, to the sleepy towns and communities with the most kind-hearted country folk.

Cattle farming remains an important source of income

History at a glance

35,000 years ago
The first native inhabitants migrate across the Bering Strait to Alaska

1492
Christopher Columbus discovers America, but thinks he has landed in the West Indies. Thus the natives are named Indians

17th Century
Five charter colonies on the East Coast: 1607 Virginia, 1620 Plymouth, 1630 Massachusetts, 1636 Connecticut and Rhode Island

1754–63
Seven Years' War in the colonies caused by conflict over fur trade

1763
Peace treaty signed in Paris. France loses its colonies in North America to England and Spain

4 July 1776
Declaration of Independence. Written by John Adams, Benjamin Franklin and Thomas Jefferson. The colonial congress secedes from the British Empire

1775–83
War of Independence. War with the British Crown erupts before the signing of the Declaration of Independence. The victory of the colonists over the 'Red Coats' greatly increases the self-confidence of the 2.5 million Americans

17 September 1787
The Constitutional Convention passes the constitution written by James Madison in Philadelphia. The constitution remains valid today. The Bill of Rights, which lists the rights of freedom, has been a model on which basic human rights worldwide have been structured

1789–97
George Washington becomes the first president of the United States. The Indians are driven from the Northwest Territory. Kentucky (1792) and Tennessee (1796) join the Union

1803
Purchase of the Ohio and Louisiana territories

1819
Florida is bought from Spain

1845
Annexation of Texas. War with Mexico results. The war ends in 1848, and the USA acquires the land that later becomes the states of New Mexico, Arizona, Colorado, Utah, Nevada and California

1861–65
The Civil War. The North is increasingly industrialized, while the huge plantations of the South remain economical through the use of slaves. When the abolitionist Abraham Lincoln is elected president, South Carolina secedes from the union, followed by ten other southern

states. They form the Confederate States of America and elect Jefferson Davis as president. The first 'modern' war with heavy automatic weapons is fought largely in the cities of the South and ends with the Confederate surrender on 9 April 1865

1867
Alaska is bought from Russia

1917
The USA enters World War I when Germany's situation improves due to the Communist Revolution in Russia

24 October 1929
On 'Black Friday', the stock market collapses. The Great Depression begins

7 December 1941
Japanese attack Pearl Harbor. Germany and Italy declare war on America

1950–53
Korean War. This is the first war in which the Super Powers of the United States and the Soviet Union face off (both are directly involved on opposite sides)

1962
Cuban missile crisis. The Soviet Union attempts to deploy medium-range atomic missiles on the Caribbean island

22 November 1963
President John F. Kennedy is assassinated in Dallas, Texas. His successor, Lyndon B. Johnson, continues Kennedy's policy of inte-gration and equal rights for Black Americans

1965–75
Vietnam War

9 August 1974
President Richard Nixon resigns as a result of the Watergate affair. During his presidency, the Republican eased relations with China and officially ended the war in Vietnam in which the U.S. became involved during the Kennedy and Johnson presidencies

1980
Ronald Reagan is elected president. Beginning of Reagan-omics (lower taxes, increased government spending) and renewed show of strength toward the Eastern Bloc

1992
Democratic candidate Bill Clinton is elected president

1995
Two federal budget crises lead to the temporary closing of national parks and the most prominent museums in Washington, D.C.

1996
Bill Clinton succeeds at what no Democrat was capable of doing for a long time: being re-elected for a second term as president

1998
A long-lasting economic boom drastically lowers the unemployment rate – the world talks about the 'American model'

Key words from A to Z

A brief summary of certain aspects of the American way of life

Brown bags

A construction worker drinking a can of beer in public, right on the street? Unthinkable! But what are the men doing over there with those brown paper bags? They're drinking beer. The cashier 'brownbagged' it for them when they bought it in the store because in many places throughout the USA, alcohol consumption is prohibited in public. Concealing a bottle in a brown paper bag makes it a bit less obvious. The person drinking hopes to escape the eagle eyes of law enforcement officers. Prohibition had a lasting effect on the issue of alcohol consumption in the United States. One pleasant side effect of Prohibition is the mixed drink, which combines alcohol with juice or carbonated beverages. The taste of the alcohol is disguised by the sweetness. Mixed drinks are available in all sorts of variations in restaurants and bars. Don't forget that each state and some individual counties even have

Patriotism is written with a capital 'P' in America

their own liquor laws. In some areas, BYO means: *bring your own!* The restaurant or bar provides cocktail shakers and ice, but you're responsible for bringing the hard stuff. In some places the alcohol even has to remain in a brown paper bag *underneath* the table. In other regions, restaurants are only allowed to serve beer and wine if more than half their turnover is from the sale of food. Nearly everywhere – except in the completely 'dry' areas – you can buy your own spirits in the Alcoholic Beverage Control (ABC) stores, liquor stores or the so-called package stores, which seem more discrete because of the name. Despite the era of Prohibition, alcohol sales per capita remain relatively high in the USA.

Campus

Even in Europe, the term *campus* has been accepted for describing the facilities of a unversity. However, the European campus, which is generally no more than a paved square with a few buildings housing lecture halls and classrooms, doesn't resemble an American university campus.

The most concrete and unmistakable examples of what a campus really is can be found among the Ivy League universities, named for their traditional, ivy-covered buildings: a republic of the learned, nearly completely closed off from the outside world and sometimes even surrounded by a wall. Most universities require first and second-year students to live on campus in *dormitories,* dwellings with rather basic furniture. Single rooms are rare, so most students have at least one roommate. The buildings of a university and maintenance costs are frequently financed by donations from former students. The libraries have an unbelievable wealth of books and the reading rooms are quiet palaces for reflecting and researching.

The architectural style of a campus is generally uniform. The students' pride for their sport teams is evident whenever games or matches are held against rival colledges or institutions. Tuition fees are extremely expensive. Yet any parent who pays the price of sending his offspring to a good university can be nearly certain that nothing else can stand in the way of his child securing a high-paying position.

Drugs

Drugs are relatively easy to buy. For this reason, Americans view drug addiction as the number one enemy, and the police force works especially hard at combatting the sale of drugs. It is important to remember that all foreigners who violate laws prohibiting the use and sale of drugs are prosecuted in the same manner as Americans. Sentences are more severe than in Europe and may even include forced labour, for example in street construction, during one's stay at the State Penitentiary.

Environment

Americans have taken steps to help reduce environmental pollution. The country was the first to ban fluorocarbons in the late '70s. The penalty for littering in some states is as high as $500. A 15-cent deposit is required in some states on each can of beverage: an effort to prevent littering. For several years recycling programmes for paper and glass products have been in operation throughout the United States.

However, concern for the environment does not prevail everywhere in the United States. For example, the Savannah River Nuclear Complex in Georgia did not observe sufficient safety standards during the manufacture of fission products for hydrogen bombs. As a result, large areas of land were exposed to long-lasting radiation.

Statistics show that the per capita use of energy in America is greater than in any other country. One reason is that energy is cheaper here than elsewhere in the world. A litre of petrol costs four times more in England than in the United States. So Americans drive everywhere – even to the park where they want to go jogging. This great use of energy also contributes to air pollution. At the same time, the laws regulating emission and recycling standards are tougher than elsewhere in the world.

Language

Because the United States is a land of immigrants, the nation's official language – English – is often spoken with diverse accents and rhythms, depending upon the region, the ancestral nationality and the ethnic diversity of the people who have settled there. New Englanders, for example, tend to speak a form of Oxford English, with clipped pronunciation. Southerners, on the other hand, draw out their words to the point where Northerners can barely understand them.

Spanish has virtually become an unofficial second language in some areas: in New York and Miami, for example. These cities have large and multinational Spanish-speaking communities. One last note: Americans tend to be quite curious and outgoing in general, particularly when they hear a new accent. Their ears will perk up and they will ask the visitor where he's from.

National Parks

The nearly 50 National Parks in the United States are among the most beautiful, the most varied, the largest and the best protected in the world. Rare animals and plants live nearly undisturbed by mankind in these wildlife preserves. One exception: despite the laws protecting national parks, one of the most famous on the East Coast, the Everglades in Florida, is being threatened by the literal draining of water. Such large areas of untouched nature are nearly impossible to find in the highly developed nations of the world. An army of park rangers joined by idealistic and very active environmental protectionists guard the parks. The park rangers are knowledgeable and friendly.

The National Parks are divided into the categories of national forests, national seashores and national recreation areas which offer camping and picnic areas. Environmental groups also work to expand the National Parks. States and individual communities have also sectioned off areas, declaring them state parks or county and community parks for private use.

The Everglades National Park in Florida

Native Americans

America's original residents most likely settled the continent 35,000 years ago, crossing the Bering Strait from Asia. They subsisted on the meat they hunted, on fish they caught and on agriculture. But they had no written language, and their craftsmanship was not as advanced as elsewhere in the world. Native Americans left their cultural imprint in the names of rivers, mountains and regions such as Apalachicola and Okeechobee in Florida. The early friendliness between the so-called Indians and the settlers from Europe soon degenerated into animosity. The breaking of peace treaties by the settlers and the systematic killing of tribes did not cease until most of the surviving Native Americans were forced to retreat to isolated reservations. Many of them still live there today.

Contemporary Native Americans are mistrustful of mainstream society but are increasingly striving to make themselves heard in local and state politics. No other minority has been less assimilated than Native Americans. However, some have managed to amass wealth. In some places, special statutes allow them to run legal gambling facilities. Others earn good wages working at construction sites for skyscrapers – since they rarely suffer from dizziness and can thus perform certain tasks better.

On the road

Americans adhere to traffic laws strictly but here, as elsewhere, there are some rules of behaviour that we would like to remind you of, which include aspects of driving that are not included in the written traffic code.

In the United States, it seems to be common knowledge that truck drivers have other things on their mind than just adhering to the speed limit. Instead, they communicate with colleagues via CB. They discuss sex, marital problems, the horse power of their rigs and, of course, the location of the next speed trap. American motorways seem to have fewer signs than European or Canadian ones. Road signs in America are also smaller, so it's a good idea to have the front-seat passenger serve as a navigator, with city map in hand.

1. If you ask for directions, you'll generally receive a description of the number of traffic lights and where to turn according to the names of streets.

2. Avoid using interstate highways for short trips near a city, especially in the East. *Toll roads* tend to be expensive, and generally run straight, which can be tedious. They are also heavily travelled. There's usually a non-toll route running parallel to nearly every toll road. However, within city limits, most interstate highways are toll-free.

3. Trust your instincts. City planning was dictated by the construction of streets, which tends to make things less complicated. What seems to be logical when trying to get from point A to point B generally works. However, street names can be similar, so take care to check the second part of the name: for example, Lincoln Road, Lincoln Street, Lincoln Place, Lincoln Drive etc.

4. Travel guides and maps are useful in finding your way, but driving into the unknown can be an adventure: every road has to lead somewhere. However, deserted streets can lead to areas of town that are best avoided.

5. If you'd like to meet interesting people for lively conversation, the best places to go are restaurants, pubs, shopping malls and churches.

6. If the driver of the car next to you starts revving his engine, don't ever take up the challenge of trying to beat him to the next traffic light – unless you're quite willing to help improve the financial situation of the town with a speeding ticket.

7. Don't ever assume that a Greyhound Bus, a truck, a vintage automobile with chrome bumpers or any automobile driven by a teenager will prematurely end its attempt at passing just because you're fast approaching from the opposite direction!

Patriotism

With waving flags and rolling drums, Americans love their country. No political party conventions take place without a sea of waving flags; no baseball games open without the crowd rising to stand and sing the national anthem. *Rally around the flag* is when American soldiers gather around the flagpole in emergencies.

Americans don't seem to mind taking jabs at themselves, sometimes making their politicians the target of sharp criticism, barbed commentary and questionable jokes. However, they do unite against outside criticism. As their saying goes: *right or wrong, it's my country.*

Politics and laws

The individual 50 states enjoy great latitude in determining their own affairs, especially in the areas of education and law. This is led to striking interstate differences. Some New England states absolutely reject the death penalty, while others regularly carry it out. The laws governing abortion also vary widely.

American individual participation in politics varies. In many communities, citizens can attend town meetings and help make decisions over the upcoming budget. A significant number of voters appear to have little faith in government: only about half of all eligible voters exercise this right – in national elections. For local elections, only about a quarter actually vote. A higher turnout does occur for a referendum. Citizens do pass a number of laws directly, such as those regarding specific taxes or the deficit limitation of the state's budget.

Religion

One of the most frequently asked questions is: *which church do you belong to?* Baptist, Methodist, Episcopalian, Latter-Day Saints (Mormon), Jewish, Roman Catholic, Muslim, countless branches of the mainline churches – the wide variety of religious affiliations has to do with the history of immigration, but also with the strict separation of Church and State. A clergyman has to see for himself how to fill the pews of his congregation. The U.S. Constitution calls for

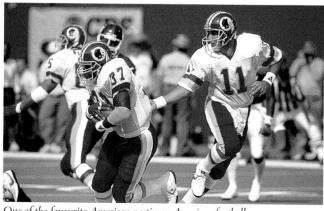

One of the favourite American pastimes: American football

the separation of Church and State, so American churches receive no direct government support. They are financed solely from the donations of their members. So the spiritual counsellor must think about ways to make his church more interesting and worth attending than the others. American church-goers are not so bound to their denomination that they wouldn't ever enter another church.

Sports

Just name a sport and you'll probably be able to find it being offered somewhere. Jai-Alai or paragliding, soccer or football, golf or squash, walking or surfing. Whether played actively or enjoyed passively, sports are the favourite pastime of most Americans. Public tennis courts that are lighted when the sun sets are no rarity; the same goes for basketball courts. Beautiful public golf courses can be used for a minimal fee. No one misses watching the live TV broadcasts of the playoffs in baseball or foot-

ball known as the *World Series* or *World Championship*. Enthusiasm for physical fitness is evident in rollerbladers, joggers and body-builders. Simple hopping on a bike or taking a walk won't do. People play sports with a great deal of dedication. Cyclists mount the newest racing bicycle made of titanium with a seat covered in kangaroo leather. Joggers wear shoes with air-filled cushions, the result of the latest studies. And who wears simple sweatsuits or cut-off T-shirts during aerobics? The outfits have turned into a market for fashion designers, each season offering more sexy creations than the last.

Weapons

Have gun, will travel. Visitors might wonder at the plethora of hand guns in private ownership in the United States. There have been many efforts to make it more difficult for private individuals to acquire arms. However, the powerful National Gun and Rifle Association has fought such attempts. This private group argues that limitations on private gun ownership infringe on a citizen's constitutional rights. Despite sinking murder rates overall, the United States still have a very high murder rate when compared to most other countries.

Women

In the New World, immigrants and settlers had no choice but to treat their wives as their equals. A woman had to stand up for herself like a man. However, women did revert to the traditional role of caretaker of the home and children when the age of prosperity emerged following the end of World War II. The '70s, but especially the '80s, following the recession, marked another turning point. It was not feminism that brought about this change, but the mandate of everyday life. The only way to be able to pay the monthly house payments and finance the second car, yes to maintain the standard of living, was for women to begin working again.

Today, more than half the positions held by professionals – generally college graduates – are in the hands of women. And outside the white-collar work force, you'll find images that surprise the average European: police women, female firefighters, female construction workers. At the very top will you still find what American women call the glass ceiling, an invisible ceiling that can only be penetrated by men seeking the highest positions. But times are changing, and today more women sucessfully

hold high ranking jobs in government and business than ever before. These women have not only achieved their own goals, the first cracks in the glass ceiling are also starting to show and are widening at such speed that some foresee a time when a woman might become president of the United States.

Xing out

Americans' sense of humour as well as everyday pragmatism can be seen in their road signs. Visitors will often see signs that consist of pictures and numbers, for example, *Ped Xing*, which stands for pedestrian crossing. (In general, wherever you see *Xing,* it means 'crossing'.) *U-turn* is another example. It stands for tur-

Gator country!

ning your car around in the street, a maneuver that is mostly forbidden. Or you might see this sign hanging in a store: *If U don't C what you need, ask 4 it.* It's easy to read these signs once you're used to them. Deciphering them can be entertaining.

Halfway around the world

*The tingling sensation of being enchanted
by unique delectables for the palate*

A pleasant discovery for European visitors is that they are greeted by a *host* or *hostess* in most restaurants, then escorted to a table. You don't just walk in and look for a place to sit, but are expected to wait politely in the foyer. A sign often requests you to *Please wait to be seated*. This way, you never have to fight over the same table with other guests. You'll never be escorted to a table until the dishes from the previous guests have been cleared away and the table has been wiped clean. If no tables are available and you have to wait, then you'll be asked – at least in better restaurants – whether you would like to proceed to the bar for a drink. Americans place emphasis on proper dress, in the better restaurants. That means: suit and tie for men, a skirt or dress and absolutely no shorts for the ladies. Again, this applies only to fancy restaurants. Otherwise, a leisurely dress code prevails. Paradoxically, no one objects if a man removes his suit coat or loosens his tie once he is seated.

The basic ingredient for crab cakes from New England

America's cuisine is as international as its population. Name a type of food and you can get it – be it Mexican, Chinese, Korean or French. The fast food restaurants remain the most inexpensive, offering primarily hamburgers, chicken or pizza. Every motorway rest stop has one or more representatives of the well-known fast-food chains, such as McDonald's, Howard Johnson's, Kentucky Fried Chicken, Pizza Hut and Taco Bell.

Chinese food is another inexpensive yet tasty alternative, as well as Thai or Vietnamese eateries. You can order food on a carryout basis, just like at the fast food restaurants. You can also have the remainder of your dinner put in a *doggy bag* or boxed to take home. Sandwiches are relatively inexpensive and available nearly everywhere: in grocery stores, drug stores, at petrol stations, delicatessens, coffee shops. However, any type of food with an ethnic flair – French, German, Italian, Spanish or classic American cuisine tends to be more expensive.

Americans have a penchant for the foods of other nations, so the dishes are usually rated good to excellent in quality. Regional, na-

23

tional or ethnic specialities create great variety in America's cuisine. For example, you have to try seafood when you're in New England. New England clam chowder, a mussel soup made with milk, cream and vegetables, is one-of-a-kind. Lobsters are abundant. Oysters, an inaffordable delicacy in Europe, are served as a side dish or as finger food with beer, comparable to a dish of pretzels or nuts. The nicest oyster cellar in the world is a snack bar – the Oyster Bar in New York's Grand Central Station.

The ecological wave has also affected many restaurants and their delivery services. An increasing number of vineyards are beginning to harvest grapes for white wine, all along the coast from New England to Virginia.

Restaurant-goers in metropolitan areas face the difficult choice of where to go. What type of food will it be tonight? Japanese? Then off to the sushi bar. German? To the Ratskeller. French? To the next brasserie. Chinese? Head for Chinatown. Greece? To the local Greek tavern. You won't find this much variety concentrated in such small geographic areas anywhere else on Earth.

Throughout the world, restaurants take great care when choosing their name to include some sort of signal to potential customers. The situation is different in the USA. A café can be an elegant dining establishment, or a simple snack bar. The best way to limit choices is to consult the Yellow Pages of the telephone book or restaurant guides available at hotels. The 'Living' or 'Style' sections of local newspapers are another good source of information on eateries.

Food critics in America who are celebrated as trendsetters give concrete information in their reviews. They list prices, recommend certain dishes and provide addresses and opening times.

Southern-style cooking is dominated by lots of rice, plenty of hot spices, chicken, ribs and, in areas where Latin American immigrants have settled, the Caribbean cuisine. An authentic Southern meal would be Southern fried chicken, black-eyed peas and cornbread. Other dishes that are just as authentic are seviche, marinated raw fish, or crabs in a sauce of lemon juice, oil, parsley and garlic. Or shrimp creole, Caribbean-style prawns, so spicy that they remind us that the consumption of hot peppers has a direct effect on body temperature!

The further away you are from the coast, the more monotonous the cuisine becomes. If you're looking for something other than classical American food, you'll begin to be disappointed in the Appalachian region. Once you get beyond the mountains, you'll find it difficult to find much of any kind of international food. So it's a good idea to fill up on breakfast, or better said, on the Western-style breakfast that has become typical even out East. A huge plate full of eggs, bacon or sausage, hash browns (fried potatoes), toast, jelly and juice. The coffee is usually served *bottomless* which does not refer to the waitresses' clothing but to the free refill offer on the coffee. It doesn't matter how many cups you drink, you can still have more. That's why lunch in the United States is a relatively small meal and dinner is eaten relatively early, around 6 pm. The evening meal is large, often consisting of meat, potatoes, salad and vegetables.

Regional cuisine in the U.S. is truly exciting in places like New Orleans or Miami. The Spaniards and later the French ruled in Dixieland. The mixture of the French and Spanish cuisine combined with Caribbean influence lead to Cajun, a sometimes extremely spicy, and relatively rich, cooking style whereby the sauces burn your tongue and the black beans mixed with rice and manioc are extremely filling.

In Miami and in the entire southern part of Florida, authentic food means whatever's Cuban, which, in turn, has its roots in Spanish food. *Tapas y mariscos*, the well-known small snacks and the exquisite seafood dishes are typical of this style. Here, contrary to other places in the United States, coffee is served hot, strong and in thimble-sized cups. For breakfast, *churros* are served, deep-fried breaded sausage. And in the evening, delicious *media-noche* sandwiches are served.

No matter what kind of regional specialities exist, one thing remains the same wherever you dine: you'll be served ice water. American beer is light in alcoholic content and served cold. Microbrews from small-sized breweries can be compared to German or other European beers. American-produced wines are often even better than some European wines.

Restaurants are divided into smoking and non-smoking sections. In some cities, restaurants are entirely non-smoking by law (as are many other public places). Defy non-smoking rules at your own risk – no doubt you will be heaped with scorn and you could get slapped with a fine ranging from $10 to $100.

Many restaurants, catering to large families (or large eaters), offer *One-Price, All-You-Can-Eat* menus. You pay one price and serve yourself from an array of main dishes and salads, all of which are often laid out buffet-style.

Service charges are rarely listed on the menu, nor is the sales tax. A state sales tax of between 7.5 to 8.5 per cent is automatically added to your bill. Tips are considered to be not so much a recognition of good service, but wages paid for work performed. A tip of around 15 percent of the net bill is considered reasonable; if you pay cash, leave the tip on the table after settling your bill. For those paying by credit card, a special box is reserved for gratuities. This is optional, of course, but if you don't add something, someone else may decide to determine the tip for you. Always ask for (and keep) your receipts.

A tip for coffee lovers is the Starbucks chain of cafés. And another hot tip for those who are especially thrifty: lots of hotels serve snacks at low prices during happy hour. When the two-for-the-price-of-one drink specials were outlawed as a result of campaigns against drunk driving, the bars thought of a new way to attract business. All you have to do is order a beer, a glass of wine or a mixed drink and you can put together a complete meal from the various snacks that are provided at certain times of the day.

Purchasing craze at sale prices

*The vast quantity of goods and excellent service
are not only tempting for Americans*

Shopping, shopping, shopping – sometimes it seems like everyone in America is constantly going shopping! Even those that really can't afford it seem to frequently succumb to the purchasing craze.

Electronic equipment is generally relatively inexpensive, when compared to prices in Europe. While it is possible to use equipment purchased in America in other countries with an adapter, be sure to get precise information before buying anything. Salesmen in America aren't necessarily informed on the cycles and watts and plugs used in Europe. Beware of photography and electronic stores that specialize in selling to tourists. There are black sheep who will sell used, outdated or incomplete equipment in the 'original packaging'. Malls are where Americans go shopping. Defining malls as mere shopping centres would be simplistic. Some look like huge concrete blocks on the outside. Once inside, you'll notice that they resemble Spanish country estates.

*Most malls are designed
to make shopping
an enjoyable experience*

The shops are surrounded by beautiful gardens, courtyards, marble floors, fountains and waterfalls; and you'll find cafés, cinemas, restaurants and hotel lobbies with live classical and pop music interspersed between the stores.

Outlet Malls, which have much less ambience, offer goods at lower prices because they're sold directly from the factory. The customer is truly king in this service-oriented society. A typical example is grocery shopping: the cashiers in a European supermarket shove the items indifferently, allowing them to pile up on top of each other. You don't know whether to start putting your groceries in bags or to pay. In an American grocery store, another worker stands behind the cashier and bags everything for you, while yet another might load the bags of groceries into your car. The situation is similar in clothing stores. You can try on as many items of clothing as you want, give just as many back, wait for the bill to be prepared and then decide not to buy anything – and the salesperson would still say *Thank you for visiting us* with a friendly smile.

Halloween and the Fourth of July

And many other events, including regional festivals

Holidays and festivals do not receive as much emphasis in America as perhaps in other parts of the world. On the other hand, some of them are so important that the world seems to stop turning. This has perhaps something to do with the fact that religion plays less of a role than the commercial aspects of certain holidays.

Trade fairs and county fairs have often been the only major event in rural areas. And since Americans don't have many vacation days (the average is two weeks a year), they go all out to enjoy long weekends. But stores remain open even on the most important holidays. Unlike in Germany, for example, where the official Christmas holidays include three days, Christmas Day is the only official holiday in the USA. But the bells of the Christmas season do toll early: the Christmas season begins during the last week of November, immediately following Thanksgiving. That's when Santa Claus figures are set up outside stores, when home owners decorate their front yards with bright lights and when 'Jingle Bells' is heard repeatedly on the radio.

The beginning of summer is marked by Memorial Day, the first long weekend at the beach, while the end of summer is marked by Labor Day, the last long weekend of the year. Thanksgiving, the harvest festival, is when families gather for the traditional feast of turkey. Other major festivals are sports events such as the *World Series,* which marks the championship in baseball, and the various football 'bowls' *(Super Bowl, Orange Bowl, etc),* which crown the champion American football teams in the college and professional leagues. Even if you're not interested in these huge sports events, it is a good idea at least to note when they occur, because the streets and public transportation systems can be hopelessly crowded.

PUBLIC HOLIDAYS

1st of January *New Year's Day*
3rd Monday in January
    Martin Luther King Day

Pumpkins are the typical symbol of Halloween

3rd Monday in February
Presidents' Day
Last Monday in May
Memorial Day
★ 4th of July
Independence Day
1st Monday in September
Labor Day
2nd Monday in October
Columbus Day
11th of November *Veterans' Day*
4th Thursday in November
★ *Thanksgiving*
25th of December
★ *Christmas*
Banks, public offices, post offices as well as some stores and restaurants are closed on official holidays.

January
Orange Bowl Classic in Miami, Florida. The greatest American football event of the Eastern League. Parades and the crowning of the Orange Bowl Queen.

February
★ *Chinese New Year* The largest Chinese communities outside of Asia celebrate the New Year according to the lunar calendar which varies from January to March. Fireworks and parades including Golden Dragons that are several hundred metres (yards) long.

MARCO POLO SELECTION: FESTIVALS

1 Chinese New Year
Wherever it's celebrated, the Far East conquers the New World: dragons and fireworks, fried duck and disguised queens (page 30)

2 Fourth of July
Everywhere you look, the Stars and Stripes sway in the wind, bright balloons, firecrackers. Families barbecue outdoors, and the heart beats even stronger for the red, white and blue (page 30)

3 Thanksgiving
The best thing to do is to be invited to join a family celebration, because this feast has to be eaten to be believed: turkey, chestnuts, corn, mashed potatoes, cranberry sauce

and, for dessert, Baked Alaska – ice cream covered with whipped cream, and then baked slightly in the oven (page 30)

4 Christmas
Starting with the first Sunday in Advent and rising to a crescendo on Christmas Eve. Bells ring and Christmas songs by Bing Crosby are heard everywhere: 'Jingle Bells' and 'We Wish You a Merry Christmas', Santa Claus singing 'Ho-ho-ho' and the clip clop of his reindeer. The commercialization of Christmas is most evident on New York's Fifth Avenue where the spending never seems to end (pages 30–31)

Caribbean atmosphere at a beach festival

March

St. Patrick's Day Irish immigrants celebrate and remember their patron saint with Irish coffee, Irish whiskey and above all with green-coloured beer – Cheers!

Mardi Gras This celebration is largely due to the Catholic population from the Caribbean in Miami and New Orleans. They passionately dance to salsa and samba rhythms. The bright sequined costumes reveal more skin than they cover up. Floats form a parade on the streets, comparable only to Latin America.

April

Spring Break This isn't actually a festival, but simply the mid-semester holiday when countless students from the East Coast migrate to the beaches of Florida to celebrate a week-long, non-stop party at the beach with drinking, dancing and show-me-what-you've-got. The main destination is Daytona Beach.

Cherry Blossom Festival The beautiful blossoms on the cherry trees attract tourists from all over the world to Washington, D.C. Japanese immigrants exhibit their calligraphy, beat on Taiko drums and perform tea ceremonies.

October

Halloween A festival mainly for children. The parents light candles inside carved pumpkins and place them on window sills to wait for the calls of the children: *Trick or treat!* Either you give the children a sweet, or they'll play a trick on you!

December

★ The Christmas season on New York's Fifth Avenue is especially beautiful and an awesome sight to behold. You can't miss the Santa Clauses in front of the department stores, which are filled with all kinds of luxury items and wonderful gifts to fulfill almost anybody's wishes.

NEW YORK

☛ City map inside back flap

(**104/C6**) What is it that makes New York so special? It's the only metropolis that truly earns this title. The one with which all other would-be metropolises are compared. Everything culminates in New York, or better said in the relatively small area of Manhattan: power, money, culture – and misery. New Yorkers show off what they possess with an air of self-confidence. And if a homeless person lying on the sidewalk is in the way, the woman in her fine fur coat simply steps over him. Because the sight of the homeless is so everyday in the Big Apple, they're called: *the uniform.* In his novel on urban life entitled *The Bonfire of the Vanities* (1987), Tom Wolfe very fittingly describes how splendour and disgrace, the art of living and violence, live side-by-side. This book falls under the genre of 'Faction' which combines fact and fiction. The content is fictitious but could be factual, all the same. Although often pronounced to be doomed, 'The Big Apple' continues to blossom anew. It seems like decades ago when the city was known for its series of postmodern skyscrapers. The *gentrification* of Manhattan, where yuppies moved, taking it over from the older established residents, is also a thing of the past. Times Square has also been transformed from a dirty and deteriorated centre of drug dealing into a renewed city centre.

SIGHTS

Brooklyn Bridge

This structure belongs to poets and painters, to the proponents of progress and architecture enthusiasts – and, last but not least, to tourists. The best time to be there is at sunrise or sunset when the skyline starts to glow in the first rays of sun of the new day or appears as a silhouette in front of the sinking ball of fire. One tip for late risers, those who prefer the sunset alternative: the *Riverside Café* on the Brooklyn side serves average-tasting food, great drinks and provides a fantastic ◁▷ view. When the neo-Gothic granite columns of the bridge were finally completed in 1883 after 16 years of construction, the steel cables carrying the suspended two-lane road and accompanying wooden pedestrian bridge were also erected. More than 150,000 people celebrated the grand opening of the bridge. Yet chief engineer John August Roebling, an immigrant from Thuringia, Germany, did not live to see this day. His leg was crushed in an accident during the initial surveying work. He died later due to complications resulting from the amputation of his leg. However, he was able to observe the construction progress of the bridge from his hospital room. His son Washington promised to complete the structure.

Central Park

Avoid the green refuge in the middle of New York at night. The park is located between 59th and 110th streets and Fifth Avenue and Central Park West (Eighth Avenue). Central Park is where office workers go during their lunch break, a seemingly boundless playground for children, a rendezvous for lovers, a favourite place for joggers, cyclists, ice skaters and rollerbladers and a showcase for worshippers of the body. New York's nouveau riches like to eat lunch at *Tavern on the Green*.

Chinatown and other districts

A bit north of Brooklyn Bridge on the Mahattan side of the river you'll find Chinatown which runs twelve blocks, starting behind City Hall. Tiny Oriental shops, snack bars, restaurants, pseudo pagodas (even the telephone booths are Oriental style), bright-coloured garlands and the Cantonese dialect of the elderly. You're looking for cheap but tasty food? This is the place! Where? Wherever you see the Chinese themselves gathered to eat. Sometimes the best eateries don't have menus in English. So, what do you do? Ask the waiter for a suggestion or see what succulent dishes the other diners are enjoying and ask for something similar. Eating in Chinatown can be a culinary adventure. The Chinese are open to eating meats that many Westerners have never tried.

Bordering on Chinatown you'll find the Bowery and the 'Street of the Forgotten' to the north. And to the east, the Lower East Side, a somewhat dangerous ghetto and simultaneously exclusive avant-garde district – an area where English is still a foreign language. Little Italy starts west of the Bowery around Grand Street. Plenty of pasta, mamma mia and pizza calzone; and then a totally different atmosphere on the other side of West Broadway, TriBeCa (*Tri*angle *Below Ca*nal Street), is a haven for artists and gallery owners. This is the place to find the 'in' bars. SoHo (*So*uth of *Ho*uston – pronounced:

Howston). The artists left this area to settle in TriBeCa when rental prices escalated. Now only the largest and profitable galleries and the most exclusive boutiques can afford to keep shop in SoHo.

Empire State Building

Begun in 1929 and completed in 1931, this structure remains the epitome of a skyscraper. The measurements: Weight: 331,120,000 kg (365,000 tonnes) Height with antenna 443 m (1462 ft). No. of stairs: 1,860; 73 elevators for those who want to avoid climbing stairs. ✇ View from the 102nd floor: approx. 80 km (50 mi). Total weight of daily visitors: impossible to estimate, nearly 36,000 people per day. Location: *5th Ave./34th St.*

Statue of Liberty

The idea was born during a dinner held at the house of French historian Edouard de Laboulaye. One of the guests, the Alsatian sculptor Frédéric-Auguste Bartholdi, had travelled to America with this idea in mind. When he arrived in New York's harbour, the vision became more concrete. Bartholdi saw a 'mighty woman bearing a torch' in his mind. The French raised $250,000; the Americans, who were only responsible for building the base for the statue to rest upon, couldn't raise a cent. 'A lighthouse in New York' – what for? Publisher Joseph Pulitzer utilized his *New York World* newspaper to launch a national fund-raising campaign. Lady Liberty illuminated the world for the first time on 28 October 1886.

Trump Tower

Donald Trump, construction investor and real estate mogul, was able to persuade financiers and property owners to support this endeavour. Trump overdid himself financially at times: divorce, an expensive mistress and failed gambling casinos in Atlantic City. Trump Tower has become an elegant symbol of the '80s, when the national and state governments and most of the American population spent more money than they earned. Fifth Avenue, shopper's paradise, begins where Trump Tower stands – on the corner of 59th Street and Fifth Avenue – and continues up to 39th Street. Some of the most expensive boutiques are located in the heart of Trump Tower, a luxury oasis covering several floors and complete with a man-made waterfall.

Wall Street

In 1653, Governor Peter Stuyvesant had a defensive wall erected to keep Native Americans away from the settlement. When the British took over the city, they no longer needed this type of protection and tore down the wall. The new street was dotted with coffee houses. The wheelers and dealers moved in when independence came – 24 merchants and auctioneers who had previously conducted business in the taverns throughout town. They decided it was time to have a base of operations and fixed opening hours – especially since $80 million in government loans were available for distribution. That's how much the War of Independence had cost the young United States. The first stock brokers chose the Tontine Coffee House on the corner of Wall Street and Water Street for their first stock exchange. Today's

New York Stock Exchange has 1,366 members and 1,700 associated companies. More than 165 million shares and securities are handled every day. Observe the market in action: the entrance to the observer's gallery is at 20 Broad Street.

Washington Square and Greenwich Village

It's been nearly four decades since the 'Village' was the centre of the Bohemians. Back in the '20s, the quarter developed into the New York version of Montmartre, where mediocre artists, radical authors and supporters of the sexual revolution gathered in brownstones. In 1960, bankers, lawyers and stock brokers discovered that living in the Village within the huge city is more pleasant than in a suburb located two hours away. The first re-urbanization began, which also later led to the acronym yuppie: *y*oung *u*rban *p*rofessional. The houses are more beautiful than ever. The theatres, bars, boutiques, restaurants and night clubs have remained in the area between Seventh Avenue and the Washington Square Park. The prices – be it for *hors d'œuvres* or a house – have tripled since then. But entertainment in the heart of Greenwich Village, Washington Square, has remained free of charge. Jugglers, poets, musicians and sometimes even political speakers gather here.

Skyscrapers

Don't limit yourself to the Empire State Building and the Trump Tower. Dozens of other skyscrapers comprising the conglomeration called Manhattan are worth seeing. The Empire State Building is only the tallest because of the antenna on top. Without that it would measure 381 m (1,238 ft). Trump Tower with its 202 m (657 ft) is a medium-range skyscraper. The list of the ten most interesting – not the highest – is as follows: Empire State Building (443 m/1,440 ft). World Trade Center (420 m/1,259 ft), Liberty/West St., *observation platform on 110th floor; Tower 2; daily 9.30am-9.30pm; admission: $4.* Chrysler Building (319 m/1,036 ft), magnificent Art Deco lobby, Lexington Ave./42nd St.; *daily 7am – 5.30pm.* Citicorp Center (279 m /837 ft), people spend their lunch hours on the plaza, Lexington Ave. between 53rd and 54th St. RCA Building (260 m/842 ft), in the Rainbow Room on the 65th floor Sat and Sun starting 12 noon, brunch, $35; and Tues-Sun starting 6pm, dinner, $50. Rockefeller Center, 5th Ave. between 48th and 51st St. World Financial Center (226 m/733 ft), the postmodern architecture of the skyscrapers in southern Manhattan, Battery Park City. AT&T Tower (198 m/644 ft), also postmodern in style, but slightly reminiscent of a monument with the round opening in the pointed gable, Madison Ave. between 55th and 56th St. Trump Tower (202 m/657 ft). IBM Tower (183 m/595 ft), classical concerts on the glass-roofed plaza during lunchtime, entrance through Trump Tower or on Madison Ave. 56th St. The Seagram Building (100 m/325 ft), which belongs to the maker of whiskey, deserves notice because it was designed by the former director of the Bauhaus in Dessau, Mies van der Rohe, Park Ave. between 52nd and 53rd St.; *Tours Tues 3pm; Tel: (212) 572-7000*

MUSEUM

The Museum of Modern Art

For a short tour of New York, the only museum we'll recommend is the 'MOMA', the world champion in exhibits of modern art. *Sat-Tues and Thurs 10.30am-6pm; Fri 10.30 am-8.30pm; Admission: $9.50; 11 West 53rd St.; Tel: (212) 708-9480*

RESTAURANTS

Indochine

Original Vietnamese cuisine with a touch of French cooking (Vietnam was a French colony). Gathering place for stars and starlets. *430 Lafayette St., near Astor Place; Tel: (212) 505-5111; Category 1*

Oyster Bar & Restaurant

Ornamental ceilings and a fresco palace in Grand Central Station. Grilled fish and a dozen different kinds of oyster. *Closed Sat and Sun; inside the train station on the 42nd St. and Park Ave. side; Tel: (212) 490-6650; Category 2*

HOTEL

Gramercy Park

There is no accommodation in New York that is simultaneously inexpensive and rated highly. You can either have high-quality rooms or a low price, but not both. The Gramercy Park Hotel is halfway affordable, not overly loud and also provides a pleasant atmosphere. *350 rooms; 2 Lexington Ave.; Tel: (212) 475-43 20; Fax: (212) 505-0535; Category 1*

You'll find more comprehensive information on the Big Apple in the MARCO POLO guide *New York*.

Indian summer and high tech

Everything has class here: the scenery, the customs and the exclusive universities

The small corner in the northeastern USA, which is about half the size of Germany, has held its place as the heart of America. Old England seems to live on between the beaches along Cape Cod, the rugged rocks of Maine, in the lonely forests of Vermont and the intellectual city of Boston. Tradition is written with a capital 'T' here. Things have class here.

New Hampshire, Massachusetts, Connecticut and Rhode Island were among the 13 states that sought independence from the British crown, going to war with Mother England to achieve independence and establish a democracy. The people of New England today remain, by and large, relatively liberal. Contributing to this liberal dominance are the so-called Ivy League universities which developed from the land grant colleges, so named because they received large tracts of land when they were founded. The term 'ivy league' was coined because of the ivy that covers the traditional brick buildings of the universities. They are, however,

Waits River, Vermont

elite because former students have contributed millions of dollars to support the universities. With this financial support, the Ivy League universities have been able to provide the most generous research scholarships, hire the best-paid professors and, as a result, select the best students.

Of course, everyone knows the names of the most famous universities in New England: Harvard, Yale and Princeton. In addition, there's the prestigious Massachusetts Institute of Technology, as well as traditional women's colleges such as Vassar and Smith. These institutes of higher learning are generally located somewhat outside the cities on a tree-covered campus. The quiet atmosphere of the classrooms, the impressive libraries and theatrical facilities invite the onlooker to begin contemplating intellectual subjects. But what would life at college be like without having a little fun? Boutiques, bars and discotheques are also plentiful, providing ample opportunities for students to spend their parents' money.

New England is also the home of the Yankees. A true Yankee is a person of few words, who tends toward Puritanism, thinks twice before spending a penny and maintains a certain amount of class arrogance. The top echelons of America's society are still dominated by what are called WASPs, White Anglo-Saxon Protestants. But if someone can prove that his roots date back to the 'Pilgrims', the first settlers who landed on the *Mayflower* at Cape Cod in 1620, then he has gained the closest thing to the status of aristocracy in the United States.

Homes in New England are built primarily of wood and are well-cared for. The classical red barns are just as much a symbol of New England as the whitewashed churches and the grey-shingled private homes. Lumber is plentiful because 70 per cent of the area of these six states consists of forests.

The rivers, which are formed from the mountain brooks, were made useful during the Industrial Age. The factories of New England produced textiles, weapons and even automobiles – the first American-made automobiles were not manufactured in the Motor City of Detroit but in Hartford, Connecticut. Traces of this former industrial boom are still evident in many places: the brick buildings of abandoned factories line the rivers; mills and dams testify to the use of water energy. The blueprints that were used to dam the Alster waterway in Hamburg were used

---

Hotel and Restaurant Prices

Hotels

Category 1: luxurious hotels and recreational facilities costing more than $200

Category 2: good hotels from $100 to $200

Category 3: simple hotels and motels under $100

Prices apply to double rooms for two people. The price of single rooms is only slightly lower. Children can generally sleep in the same room with their parents at no extra cost. All hotels and motels have telephones and televisions in the rooms. Many also have a swimming pool.

Inexpensive motel chains such as Best Western, Days Inn or Econo Lodge are generally located on busy streets or motorways.

Restaurants

Category 1: more than $50
Category 2: from $30 to $50
Category 3: less than $30

The prices apply to dinners including soup or an appetizer, an entrée and dessert.

Abbreviations

Ave.	Avenue
St.	Street
Blvd.	Boulevard

MARCO POLO SELECTION: NEW ENGLAND

1 John F. Kennedy Library
Impressive memorial for the assassinated president (page 41)

2 Mount Washington Cog Railway
The oldest cog railroad in the world still operates (page 43)

3 Castles in Newport
The palaces of America's financial aristocrats; open to the public (page 44)

4 Whale Watching
Visit with the peaceful giants of the ocean (pages 41, 43)

---

to design the dam for the Charles River in Boston.

ACADIA NATIONAL PARK

(105/F3) The only National Park in New England and the only one on the Eastern Seaboard is located in Maine. Covering a total area of 150 sq. km (94 sq. miles), the park includes large portions of Mount Desert Island, Schoodic Peninsula and the Isle au Haut. A unique combination of quiet forests and waves crashing against the granite cliffs, the bright fishing harbours and small holiday resort villages. The main attraction on the island is Bar Harbor, where the well-to-do used to flock for summer holidays. The higher mountains are located on the eastern part of the island; the top of Cadillac Mountain (467 m/1,518 ft) can be reached by car. The ◁▷ view is breathtaking!

HOTELS

Ledgelawn Inn
An old cottage with fireplaces in the rooms and a 'Widow's Walk',

a ◁▷ look-out platform. *33 rooms; 66 Mount Desert St., Bar Harbor; Tel and Fax: (207) 288-4596; Category 1-2*

BENNINGTON

(104/C4) With its quaint white houses, surrounded by white picket fence, and small church, this New England town seems like it was taken straight out of a picture book (pop. 16,000). It's also the ideal starting point for an excursion into the south of Vermont. The rolling hills are especially beautiful in the autumn. Thus Vermont is a popular spot for the 'fall colours' tourists. The *Bennington Museum* is also worth visiting, featuring the world's largest collection of naive paintings by Grandma Moses. Bennington is located about 50 km (31 miles) east of Albany.

BERKSHIRE HILLS

(104/C4-5) The Berkshires, a set of hills running north to south, is an area in the western part of Massachusetts where literary figures, musicians and actors retreated in the 19th century when the Boston summers became too steamy. Obviously, the reason they came here was to enjoy the charming and refreshing scenery. The towns of *Stockbridge* and *Lenox* are real treasures. The open-air museum *Hancock Shaker Village* demonstrates to visitors how the Shakers, a religious denomination also known for the beautiful simplicity of their furniture, lived and worked. Numerous festivals take place during the summer in the Berkshires; the Boston Symphony Orchestra has its summer concert series in *Tanglewood*.

RESTAURANTS

The Candlelight Inn

The food served here combines the best New England traditions with elements of the modern American cuisine (also a hotel with 8 rooms). *Lenox, 53 Walker St.; Tel: (413) 637-1555; Category 2*

INFORMATION

Berkshire Hills Visitors Bureau
Berkshire Common, Pittsfield; MA 01201; Tel: (413) 443-9186

BOSTON

☛ City map inside back flap

(**105/D4**) The Massachusetts state capital is the most important and largest New England city (pop. 2.8 million) and after New York, the most prominent financial centre on the East Coast. Boston was hit relatively hard in the last recession, but the quality of life remains high here. The downtown area is manageable very well on foot. With red brick buildings, narrow alleys and many green areas, Boston is similar to London, Amsterdam or Lübeck in Germany.

Boston was founded in 1630 by the Puritans. The city quickly gained prominence as a trade

The Old Cobblestone Street in Boston

centre owing to its location on the Charles River. The Bostonians played a key role in the fight of the colonies for independence from the British. Nearly all of the historical sights in this city deal with the Revolutionary War period.

SIGHTS

Back Bay
A generous-sized residential area with buildings from the second half of the 19th century. Borders on *Copley Square* with the John Hancock Tower (outook platform), Trinity Church and the Boston Public Library.

Beacon Hill
The charm of Boston's brick homes comes to life in this traditional residential area north of the Common.

Freedom Trail
This trail marked by a red line on the sidewalk leads to all the sites from the Revolutionary War period. The trail starts at the *Common*, the main city park (at the tourist information booth).

MUSEUMS

Computer Museum
The only museum in the world which deals exclusively with computers. *Daily 10am-5pm, winter: closed Mon; Admission: $7; 300 Congress St.; Tel: (617) 426-2800*

John F. Kennedy Library
★ Museum and memorial for the American president who was assassinated in 1963. The memorial also honours his brother Robert who was killed a few years later. The spectacular building was designed by I. M. Pei. *Daily 9am-5pm; Admission: $6; south of downtown in Dorchester; Tel: (617) 929-4523*

Museum of Fine Arts
Paintings by European and American artists. *Tues-Sun 5pm-9.45pm, Wed 4pm-9.45pm; Admission: $7; 465 Huntington Ave.; Tel: (617) 267-9300*

TOURS

Whale Watching
★ The New England Aquarium offers whale watching tours in the summer. *Central Wharf; Tel: (617) 973-5200*

RESTAURANTS

Durgin Park
Loud atmosphere. Large portions. Excellent prime rib, fresh lobster stew. *340 Faneuil Hall Marketplace; Tel: (617) 227-2038; Category 3*

Legal Sea Foods
Famous for their fish and seafood. *35 Columbus Ave.; Tel: (617) 426-4444; Category 2*

SHOPPING

You'll find all kinds of stores at *Quincy Market* between Congress Street and the Waterfront. *Filene's Basement, a department store known for its low prices (426 Washington St.)*

HOTELS

Bed and Breakfast Associates Bay Colony
Agency that books accommodation in Bed & Breakfasts and small flats. *Babson Park Branch;*

Tel and Fax: (617) 449-5302; Category 2–3

Copley Plaza
Centrally located grand hotel. *370 rooms; 138 St. James Ave.; Tel: (617) 267-5300; Fax: 247-6681; Category 1*

INFORMATION

Greater Boston
Convention and Visitors' Bureau
Prudential Plaza; P.O. Box 490, Boston MA 02199; Tel: (617) 536-4100

SURROUNDING AREA

Cambridge   (105/D4)
The city on the opposite side of the Charles River is the home of two famous universities: the Massachusetts Institute of Technology (MIT) and Harvard University, the oldest college in the USA. Students offer free tours of the campus. Harvard also houses a number of excellent museums.

Concord/Lexington   (105/D4)
These two quaint towns on the western edge of Boston played a major role in the fight for independence. This is where the Americans fired the first shots against the British. During the 19th century, Concord rose to become the literary centre of the USA. The houses where Emerson, Thoreau and Hawthorne lived and worked can be toured.

Old Sturbridge Village   (105/D4)
This open-air museum located 80 km (50 miles) west of Boston propels you back into the 19th century. Walking through the village, you'll meet people who are not only clothed in the attire of that time, but also demonstrate how their ancestors lived and worked.

Plymouth Plantation   (105/E5)
In 1620, the *Mayflower* brought a group of British settlers to America. These settlers founded the first permanent European settlement in the New World: Plymouth. The village museum is a reconstruction of this settlement. Anchored on the coast you'll find a full-size replica of the *Mayflower*.

CAPE COD

This Massachusetts peninsula extends about 100 km (63 miles) out into the Atlantic Ocean. The long sandy beaches and hundreds of hotels and restaurants make Cape Cod a favourite weekend and holiday destination. However, it's still possible to find a quiet place to imagine what it was like when the painters moved to the quaint city of *Provincetown* at the beginning of the 20th century. They were captivated by Cape Cod. The *Cape Cod National Seashore* is a wildlife preserve with a series of sand dunes extending several kilometres. The islands of *Martha's Vineyard* and *Nantucket* (ferry crossing), located just off Cape Cod, are also favourite holiday destinations for New Englanders.

MUSEUMS

Heritage Plantation of Sandwich
Several museums are joined by a beautiful park which showcase old-fashioned cars, artwork, folkcraft and military history.

Summer: daily 10am-5pm; Admission: $7; Sandwich, Grove/Pine St.; Tel: (508) 888-3300

TOURS

Provincetown Whale Watch

★ Boat excursions to look for whales during summer migration. *Admission: $18, children under 9 free; mid-June-Labor Day 8.30 & 11.30 am, 2.30 & 5.30 pm; 132 Bradford St.; Tel: (508) 487-3322*

INFORMATION

Cape Cod Chamber of Commerce

P.O. Box 16, Hyannis, MA 02601; Tel: (508) 362-3225

LOWELL

(**104/C4**) The city at the fork of the Concord and Merrimack rivers was the birthplace of the Industrial Revolution in America. Francis C. Lowell built his first factory here which was equipped with mechanical looms, in 1813. A short time later, the city of Lowell became a major centre of the textile industry – and the battlefield for union struggles. Following World War I, many of the spinning mills were closed. Large parts of the city have recently been restored.

MUSEUMS

Lowell National Historical Park

Spinning mills, the workers' dwellings, out-dated water power plants as well as numerous exhibitions in the historical factories document the early days of the Industrial Revolution. Tours conducted by the park ranger. *Daily 8.30am-5pm; Admission free; 246 Market St.; Tel: (508) 459-1000*

MOUNT WASHINGTON

(**105/D3**) The highest peak in New England is Mount Washington in the White Mountains of New Hampshire – 1,917 m (6,230 ft). The breathtaking ◀▶ view from the top of the surrounding mountains and forests is worth the climb. For those who don't want to conquer the mountain on foot, the ★ *Mount Washington Cog Railway* has been creeping up the steep mountain (37% grade) since 1869. The best starting point for tours of the mountains is Bretton Woods, Conway or neighbouring North Conway. Franconia Notch, Crawford Notch and Pinkham Notch (notches are gorges) are also worth a stop. Beautiful hiking trails are located here. The route along the Kancamagus Highway, located west of Conway, is especially scenic in the autumn owing to the woods along the road.

NEW BEDFORD

(**105/D5**) Whale harpooning was the primary industry in New England at the beginning of the 19th century, and the centre of whaling was in New Bedford, Massachusetts, where the ships were anchored. Various subcontracting industries blossomed simultaneously. Herman Melville's *Moby-Dick* was set here; the well-known story of the hunt for the white whale starts in New Bedford.

MUSEUMS

Whaling Museum

The best collection anywhere on the subject of whaling. An original whaling boat is exhibited in the centre of the museum. *Daily 9am-5pm, Thurs 9am-8pm; Admission: $3.50; 18 Johnny Cake Hill; Tel: (508) 997-0046*

NEW HAVEN

(**104/C5**) The main reason to visit New Haven, Connecticut, is to see Yale University, one of the country's most elite colleges. Since its founding in 1701, Yale has competed with Harvard to see which university can boast of more Nobel Prize winners and top politicians. Students give free tours of the campus. Excellent museums, especially interesting is the *Beinecke Rare Book and Manuscript Library*.

SURROUNDING AREA

Mystic Seaport   (**104/C5**)
The large open-air museum east of New London gives visitors an idea of what life was like in a typical harbour city in New England. You can tour historical workshops and homes, board boats and view exhibitions on the shipping industry. *Daily 9am-5pm, after Columbus Day 10am-4pm; Admission: adults $16, children 6 to 12 years $7.50; Tel: (860) 572-5315 or (888) 973-2767*

NEWPORT

(**105/D5**) Newport, Rhode Island, has something you would never expect to see in America: ★ Castles! Built at the end of the 19th century by the financial aristocrats: the Vanderbilts, the Morgans, the Astors, etc, spent the summer months here in these palatial structures along the Atlantic shore. Thanks to the Newport Preservation Society, the most spectacular 'cottages', such as *The Breakers* and *Marble House*, are maintained for public viewing. A stroll along *Cliff Walk* provides a view of the palaces from the ocean side.

RESTAURANTS

The Mooring
❧ Good fish and lobster with a view of the harbour, drinks on the veranda. *Sayer's Wharf; Tel: (401) 846-2260; Category 2*

PORTLAND

(**105/E3**) With its population of 65,000 people, Portland is the largest city in Maine and an important harbour. Like many other cities in New England, Portland boomed during the '70s; this economic era is noticeable throughout the city: the Victorian section of the city *Old Port Exchange* with its stores and restaurants is a fine example of successful urban renewal. In addition to historical homes, such as the Victoria Mansion, the *Portland Museum of Art*, which specializes in 19th- and 20th-century American art, is also definitely worth a visit.

SURROUNDING AREA

Maine Coast   (**105/E3–4**)
The most impressive part of the New England coast begins north of Portland. There you'll find a forested, jagged coastline with lengthy bays harbouring quaint fishing towns, such as *Bath* and *Boothbay Harbor*. To the south you'll find sandy beaches. The

Lighthouse near Portland, Maine

picturesque town of *Kennebunkport* is located about 40 km (25 miles) south of Portland. This is where former U.S. President George Bush owns a summer cottage. Yet his visits there no longer attract as many onlookers.

SALEM

(**105/D4**) This small town (pop. 37,000) along the coast north of Boston has become infamous for the persecution of witches: in 1692, women accused of being witches were burned at the stake in Salem. The strict Puritans, who dictated public life back then, condemned 19 people to death by hanging because they had formed a 'pact with the devil'. The *Salem Witch Museum* features a historically accurate and well-done multimedia show on the subject. The *Peabody Museum* shows another major aspect of this quaint city which was once one of the most important harbours on the Atlantic. The exhibits cover the maritime background of the city. The magnificent *mansions on*

Chestnut Street are evidence of the wealth the merchants were able to accumulate.

WOODSTOCK

(**105/D3**) Woodstock (not to be confused with *the* Woodstock where the famous rock festival was held and which later became the symbolic climax of the flower children movement and hippie era) is one of the model villages in Vermont: Victorian homes made of wood and stone line the green, as New England city squares are called. A typical covered wooden bridge leads cars over the Ottauquechee River. The *Billings Farm Museum* at the northern edge of the village reveals the life of Vermont farmers during the 19th century.

HOTELS

Woodstock Inn and Resort
Traditional and classy hotel on the green, where tennis and golf can be enjoyed. *146 rooms; 14 The Green; Tel: (802) 457-1100; Category 1*

SURROUNDING AREA

Green Mountains (**104/C4**)
Woodstock is a good starting point, if you have an excursion into the Green Mountains in mind. This scenic range extends through Vermont from north to south. *Brandon Gap* and the *Middlebury Gap* are easily integrated as part of this day trip (good hiking trails). Also stop at the nice towns of *Brandon, Cornwall, Lower Grandville* and *Hancock.*

Vibrant cities and open country

Political and economic power collide – from New York to Washington, D.C.

John Dos Passos said it fittingly, 'If you can get bored in New York then you're in poor shape'. The author was talking about the city. Yet the Big Apple with its 120 skyscrapers is not the only attraction the state of New York has to offer. It takes awhile to get away from the fully packed expressways. But anyone who has managed to make it across the Long Island Expressway to the Hamptons knows why members of New York's jet set flee to this area in the summertime. You'll find traditional and quaint ambience in this village and the nearby polo clubs and golf courses. Yet the main attraction of this 'long island' is the surprisingly empty beach, despite the proximity to the city. Mother Nature must have decided that New York needed another natural attraction at the other end of the state. For a truly spectacular natural wonder is located in the northwest corner of the state: Niagara Falls. The Niagara River, which connects Lake Erie with Lake Ontario, is only 55 km (34½

The symbol of power: the Capitol in Washington, D.C.

miles) long. But up to 7,000 cubic metres (247,000 cubic ft) of water tumble down the Horseshoe Falls and the American Falls. Together they form a double veil of mist that is best viewed from the boat *Maid of the Mist*. In 125,000 years, this natural spectacle will no longer exist, because the water from the rocky promontories sinks annually by about 30 cm (12 in.).

New Jersey calls itself the 'Garden State', and it's true that large portions of this state, which borders on New York, consist of green suburbs. B&T's — that's what New Yorkers call the people from the other side of the Hudson River: Bridge and Tunnel People. Yet New Jersey has one up on New York: gambling is legal in Jersey's Atlantic City. So New Yorkers migrate there in crowds, by bus or helicopter. The beach town with its classic boardwalk has become a kind of mecca for gambling.

In contrast, Pennsylvania offers more tranquil destinations. Philadelphia, the most important city in Pennsylvania, where the Declaration of Independence was signed and the Constitution

47

passed, and Gettysburg is the site of the first battle of the Civil War. In the Pennsylvania Dutch Country, people are not descendants of Dutch but of German immigrants ('deutsch' changed to 'dutch') from the Rhineland Palatinate area. Yet the area is most well known for the Amish people, also descendants of German immigrants. This religious group, concentrated in Lancaster, York and Strasburg, rejects any form of modern technology. Kerosene lamps light their homes, and horse-drawn carriages are the means of transportation.

The best Maryland offers are the crabs that are caught in the deep waters of Chesapeake Bay. The largest city in Maryland is Baltimore, one of the three oldest metropolitan areas next to Boston and New York. Until recently, the only tourists who toured Baltimore were on the trail of the cleptomaniac Marnie – Tippi Hedren from Alfred Hitchcock's psychothriller by the same name. But that has changed. Regular tourists are also now wandering through the harbour of this former tobacco trade centre.

The District of Columbia, the nearly square section of land that forms the U.S. capital, is located between Maryland and Virginia, where the southern states begin. This symbol of world power is full of obelisks, neoclassical temples and a fantastic museum mile as part of the Mall which, in this case, does not stand for a shopping centre, but for the broad boulevard in the middle of the government district. You just can't miss this veritable world capital.

ANNAPOLIS

(**109/E1**) The quaint, small town (pop. 33,000), located about 50 km (31 miles) east of Washington, D.C., is the capital of the state of Maryland. Although Annapolis has retained much of its colonial charm, the five million tourists who pour through the city's narrow streets do not help to evoke the peaceful atmosphere one would imagine. Worth visiting are the famous *Marine Academy,* the *Maryland State House* and the *Hammond-Harwood House* (1774).

SURROUNDING AREA

St. Mary's City (109/E2)

This small town south of Annapolis is not as well known among tourists and thus a less crowded place to discover the charm of Chesapeake Bay.

ATLANTIC CITY

(109/F1) What Las Vegas is in the desert is Atlantic City on the ocean: a gambler's paradise. The roulette ball has been allowed to roll here since 1976, and the one-armed bandits are allowed to captivate anyone willing to keep feeding them coins. If the state of New Jersey had not granted the gambling license to Atlantic City, the once famous holiday resort would have deteriorated. Today, the casino strip along the beach of the city of 40,000 is a popular weekend destination for gamblers from New York and Philadelphia.

SIGHTS

The Boardwalk

❖ The casinos lining the wooden planks of the beach promenade try to outdo each other to attract gamblers. The tackiest is Donald Trump's Taj Mahal, opened in 1990.

BALTIMORE

(109/E1) The largest city of the state of Maryland (pop. 2.3 million) is located on the northern arm of Chesapeake Bay. Baltimore is one of the surprises awaiting visitors to the East Coast. The former manufacturing centre, known for its ship-building industry, has become quite attractive owing to an exemplary city renovation programme. The city boasts numerous art museums.

The National Aquarium in Baltimore, Maryland

Inner Harbor

Restaurants and stores, old ships and museums, boat rentals and a 'water taxi' which docks at all the sites lining the harbour.

National Aquarium

★ The most interesting aquarium by far in all of America! Featuring a huge tank with a glass tunnel, surrounding visitors with sharks, fish, turtles and more than 5,000 other sea animals. *Sat–Thurs 9am-5pm, Fri 9am-8pm; Admission: $11.95, children 3 to 11 years $7.50; Tel: (410) 576-3800*

Baltimore Area Convention Visitors' Association

300 West Pratt St., Baltimore, MD 21201; Tel: (410) 837-4636

PHILADELPHIA

(104/B6) 'The city of brotherly love', Philadelphia (pop. 6 million in the greater metropolitan area) competes with Boston for the role of the most historic city in the USA. This is where the Declaration of Independence was written and signed. The Continental Congress convened here. Philadelphia was the U.S. capital before the government moved to Washington, D.C.

The main sights date back to colonial times. In addition, Philadelphia is an ethnically colourful city offering lots of entertainment opportunities in the evening. Despite its proximity to New York, Philadelphia has maintained its standing.

'America's most historic square mile'

Worth seeing in the Independence National Historic Park are the Liberty Bell, Independence Hall and other buildings that played a role in the fight for independence. What has remained important to Americans also provides Europeans with something to which they can relate: the American historical experience.

Society Hill

A traditional, lovingly restored residential area extending between Walnut and South St., 9th and Front St.

Philadelphia Museum of Art

One of the most important art collections in the United States. *Tues-Sun 10am-5pm; Admission: $6, Sun free; Benjamin Franklin Parkway/26th St.*

Rodin Museum

The largest collection of pieces by French sculptor Auguste Rodin outside Paris. *Tues-Sun 10am–5pm; Admission: $1; 22nd St./Benjamin Franklin Parkway*

Jim's Steaks

Offering the typical Philadelphia cheese steaks. *400 South St.; Tel: (215) 928-1911; Category 3*

PhilaDeli

Quaint diner with nice atmosphere frequented by local residents. *410–412 South St.; Tel: (215) 923-1986; Category 3*

SHOPPING

Italian Market
A bustling street market reminiscent of Naples: textiles, food, curios, household and miscellaneous items are traded or sold in a lively atmosphere. *9th St. north of Wharton St.*

HOTELS

Rittenhouse
Well-managed, modern luxury hotel in a wonderful location. *98 rooms; 210 West Rittenhouse Square; Tel: (215) 546-9000; Fax: 732-3364; Category 1*

ENTERTAINMENT

❖ Popular area is South Street east of 7th St.; restaurants, bars, trendy shops. Events take place on a regular basis at Penn's Landing. Several dance bars and clubs are located on the wharfs north of Penn's Landing.

INFORMATION

Philadelphia Visitor Center
16th St./John F. Kennedy Blvd., PA 19102; Tel: (215) 636-1666 or (800) 321-9563

SURROUNDING AREA

Amish Country   (104/A–B6)
About an hour's drive west of Philadelphia, you'll find *Lancaster,* the most important city in Amish Country. The adherents of this religious group came to Pennsylvania at the end of the 17th century and continue to live the traditional lifestyle. Please note that many Old-Order-Mennonites do not wish to be photographed. *Visitor Center, 501 Greenfield Rd.; Tel: (717) 299-8901*

PITTSBURGH

(103/E5) The historical centre of this city is located at the 'Golden Triangle', formed by the Monongahela, Allegheny and Ohio rivers. The city's name is nearly synonymous with steel since Pittsburgh advanced to become the world's largest manufacturing centre of steel! The second largest city of Pennsylvania (pop. 2.2 million) has shaken off the image of dust and cinders and, since the '80s, has been going through a period of renaissance. The steel giants of Carnegie and Frick left an inheritance for the cultural atmosphere in Pittsburgh: the *Carnegie* museumcomplex and the *Frick Art Museum.*

WASHINGTON, D.C.

☛ **City map inside back flap**
(109/D–E1) Voilà, the country's capital! A symphony of white marble, neo-classical buildings, broad park areas and waterways that reflect the green and white of the many trees. Washington, D.C., was created to serve as the nation's capital: in 1790, the swamp area of the Potomac River was drained, and the first president moved into the newly erected White House in 1800. Tourists, government officials, journalists and businessmen dominate the atmosphere of this city of nearly 600,000 residents. The city offers a wide variety of sights and excellent museums that are free, and the Georgetown area offers a first-class nightlife.

SIGHTSEEING

The best place to start a walking tour is on Capitol Hill, located at the eastern end of the Mall. Towering above all else here is the *United States Capitol* (guided tours); behind that is the *Supreme Court,* the nation's highest court, and the *Library of Congress,* the largest library in the world *(guided tours).* The Mall, a 3.2-km (2- mile) long strip of green land which runs between the Capitol and the *Lincoln Memorial,* and the large national museums of the *Smithsonian Institution* are located on either side of the Mall. From the *Washington Monument,* a 169-m (550-ft) tall obelisk (elevator), you'll have a breathtaking ⬇ view over the entire city. Turning away from the obelisk and walking north, you'll arrive at the *White House,* the president's residence *(guided tours).*

The neo-classical monuments include the memorials for presidents Lincoln and Jefferson. New among the memorials is the one for Franklin Delano Roosevelt. For many visitors, the ★ *Vietnam Veterans' Memorial* is the most moving monument. This black stone wall is engraved with the names of 58,132 American soldiers killed and declared missing during the U.S. involvement in Indochina in the '60s.

Arlington Cemetery
The final resting place for national heroes, the Arlington Cemetery, is located on the other side of the Potomac and, quite logically, not far from the Pentagon. The graves of John F. Kennedy and Jackie Kennedy Onassis are also here. *In summer 8am-7pm, Admission free*

MUSEUMS

Dumbarton Oaks
A special treat for lovers of Byzantine art. The park around the museum is also worthwhile. *Tues–Sun 2–5pm, Gardens daily 2–6pm; Admission: Gardens, $4; 1703 32nd St. NW; Tel: (202) 339-6400*

Smithsonian Institution
Nearly all the museums flanking the Mall are part of the Smithsonian Institution, the foundation started by a rich Englishman. The most interesting museums are the ★ *National Air and Space Museum (daily 10am–5.30pm),* which contains fascinating exhibits on the space programme, and the *National Gallery of Art. Mon–Sat 10am–5pm, Sun 11 am–6pm; Admission free; Tel: (202) 357-2700*

United States Holocaust Memorial Museum
An especially moving representation of the history of Jewish persecution and genocide, the history of the fascist Nazi regime and the resistance against Hitler's dictatorship. *Daily except for Yom Kippur and 25 Dec 10am-5.30pm, Admission free; however, tickets must be booked in advance due to great popularity: either at the entrance for the same day or at Ticketmaster, 100 Raoul Wallenberg Place SW; Tel: (202) 488-0400*

RESTAURANTS

I Ricci
❋ This popular Trattoria serves northern Italian cuisine and attracts well-heeled customers. *1220 19th St.; Tel: (202) 835-0459; Category 1*

The National Air and Space Museum in Washington, D.C.

Vietnam Georgetown Restaurant

You can dine outside in a nice garden in the summer. The food is inexpensive and tasty. *2934 M St. NW; Tel: (202) 337-4536; Category 3*

The Latham

Unbeatable owing to its superb location: the quaint mid-class hotel is situated in Georgetown. *143 rooms; 3000 M St. NW; Tel: (202) 726-5000; Fax: 337-4250; Category 2*

Ritz Carlton

Old elegant hotel near Dupont Circle and the embassies. *230 rooms; 2100 Massachusetts Ave.; Tel: (202) 293-2100; Fax: 293-0641; Category 1*

The place to be if you're looking for the nightlife in Washington, D.C., is 'M Street' in the nice quarter of ✪ *Georgetown* and specifically the M St./Wisconsin Ave. corner. Yet the nightlife in Washington is not exactly overwhelming. Things liven up at *Adams Morgan,* in the area around Columbia Rd. and 18th St. which attracts a more ethnically mixed crowd,

Washington, D.C., Convention and Visitors' Association

1455 Pennsylvania Ave. NW, D.C. 20005; Tel: (202) 789-7037

Mt. Vernon   (109/D1)

George Washington's country home, a beautiful mansion with guided tours, can easily be reached from the city by boat. The nautical journey on the Potomac is one of the most impressive experiences of this day excursion. *Departure from Pier 4, 6th/Water St.*

Shenandoah National Park   (109/D1-2)

To reach this stunning park, drive west on I-66. ⬦ *Skyline Drive,* a panoramic street, which begins at Front Royal, provides a wonderful view of the Shenandoah River Valley and the Blue Ridge Mountains. There are also hiking trails. As part of this excursion you must include a visit to the ★ *Luray Caverns,* limestone caves with beautiful stalactites.

Faded and revived greatness

The high-tech and media industries are booming in the South

Gone with the wind? Atlanta is the setting of the book about the downfall of the South and also where the movie *Gone with the Wind* was filmed. Yet, the quintessence of the good old South is everything but a museum of the plantation era. During the Civil War, in 1864, General Sherman, the commander of the Union (northern) Army, kept the city surrounded for 117 days. By the time Atlanta was captured, 90 percent of the city's buildings were nothing but smouldering rubble. Since then it has been attractively rebuilt. Atlanta has the second largest airport in the world. It is headquarters of the global TV network CNN and the first major southern city to elect an Afro-American mayor. A unique architectural and sociological transformation has taken place along Peachtree Street, where Scarlett O'Hara's heart beat faster. Peachtree Center, which comprises nearly the entire downtown area, has developed into one singular complex of skyscrapers connected by bridges, walkways and underground malls. Anyone doing business here leaves his or her car in one of the parking garages. This entire complex is privately owned. Life in this complex is impossible to imagine without air conditioning. Private guards maintain law and order and keep unwelcome visitors outside this artificial city-within-a-city.

If you're looking for images of the Deep South — classical mansions with columns and porticoes lining the screened-in verandas, with Spanish moss hanging from the oak trees, rolling hills and the rolling southern dialect — then you have to look outside the cities that generally stand for the South: Columbia, South Carolina; Durham, North Carolina; Richmond, Virginia – these communities have all followed Atlanta's modern-day example, albeit not as extremely.

The 11 states that seceded from the Union in 1860 to form the Confederacy and did not begin lifting racial segregation until well into the '60s have profited from a migration in the past two decades. (This chapter refers to Virginia,

A remnant of an important business from the past: the old cotton exchange in Savannah, Georgia

55

MARCO POLO SELECTION: THE SOUTH

1 Cape Hatteras
The highest dunes on the Atlantic beaches of North Carolina (page 62)

2 CNN Center
Where the entire world can view the entire world at the touch of a button (page 57)

3 Savannah
The most beautiful city of the Old South along the coast of Georgia (page 62)

4 University of Virginia
The university founded by Thomas Jefferson in Charlottesville (page 61)

the Carolinas and Georgia.) Millions of people apparently decided to flee the four changing seasons in the North to live and work in the heat of the South. The so-called Sunshine Economy resulted. The Japanese automobile giants Nissan and Honda built factories; Ford and General Motors transferred their most modern production facilities to the South; BMW also opened a plant here.

For remnants of the real Good Old South, visitors will have to look beyond the beaten path of tourist attractions and the large cities with nostalgic names. Note the thoroughbreds of millionaire horse breeders grazing on the rolling hills of Virginia. Or stop by the beautiful campus of the University of Virginia, founded by Thomas Jefferson in Charlottesville. No other city radiates the sweet humid air of the South more than Savannah (the Beach Boys sang the following lines about this city: *I was down in Savannah, eating cream and banana, when the heat just made me faint).* Founded as the 'first modern city' of the continent in 1733, Savannah remains essentially unchanged. The streets were carefully designed on a pattern of uniform grids. However, no two buildings are the same. Savannah is the incarnation of the Deep South.

The Atlantic coast provides fascination of another kind: Cape Hatteras, which boasts the highest dunes in the world. This is where the Wright brothers made their first test flights. Even during the main tourist season, you'll find a surprising amount of peace and quiet here.

ATLANTA

(**111/F2**) Margaret Mitchell's Atlanta lives on only in her book and the movie. The author died in 1949 at age 48. She was hit by a car on her beloved Peachtree Street.

Doc Pemberton's Atlanta flows around the entire globe: in 1886 he invented a caffeinated beverage called Coca-Cola.

Martin Luther King Jr.'s Atlanta has undergone changes: his freedom marches helped put an end to Jim Crow, which was the system of racial segregation, and paved the way for black Americans to advance to some of the highest public offices in the country. A large number of Afro-Americans has not been able to break out of the lower income brackets, but King remains a role model and an inspiration for young American blacks who aspire to personal achievement and social change. King was awarded the Nobel Peace Prize and later assassinated in a hotel in Memphis in 1968.

Ted Turner's Atlanta doesn't even seem to exist, at least not in the news reports of his Cable News Network (CNN). The remarkably small-sized team of producers at CNN is told not to concentrate on local or national news, much less the city from which they broadcast, but to portray the 'global village' Ted Turner helped to create.

John Portman. Who? John Portman: his Atlanta is reality; the architect has revolutionized the construction of hotels. He invented the style that has influenced all other buildings in Atlanta. A simple summary: a 20 to 70-storey building rises above a covered courtyard, with balconies that look out over it, glass elevators that ascend the sides of the building and a huge patio on the ground floor, which is filled with restaurants and boutiques.

Georgia Peach: her Atlanta is as omnipresent as any fictitious figure; Georgia Peach isn't a specific girl but a catchall for full-figured, young blonde women with rosy complexions, supposedly more beautiful than all other American women.

SIGHTS

CNN Center
★ Ultra-modern office and hotel complex that also houses CNN's studios. Forty-five-minute tour of the broadcasting facilities. *Daily 9am-6pm, hourly tours (reservations preferred!); Admission: $7, Marietta St./Techwood Dr.; Tel: (404) 827-2307*

Martin Luther King Jr. National Historic Site
Archives, library, birthplace, grave and the Ebenezer Baptist Church of the slain African-American pastor and civil rights leader. *Daily 10am-5pm, summer until 8pm; Admission free; 449 Auburn*

The CNN Center in Atlanta

Ave. near Dr. Charles Allen Dr.; Tel: (404) 524-1956

Peachtree Center
The futuristic office complex and most spectacular product of modern architecture with the tallest hotel in the world, the 73-floor Westin Hotel, a luxurious mall and interior gardens. *Daily; Admission free, on Karree Baker, Ellis, Williams and Courtland St.; Tel: (404) 614-5000*

Underground Atlanta
Under the new city you'll find a maze of alleys, narrow cobblestone streets and buildings that survived the great fire of 1864. During the Civil War battle for Atlanta, the entire area was one huge field hospital. The area was reopened in 1989 as a town centre, featuring exhibitions, restaurants, nightclubs and street artists. *Daily; Admission free; Alabama St./Central Ave.; Tel: (404) 523-2311*

The World of Coca-Cola Pavilion
When the publicist H. L. Mencken ridiculed the South back in the '30s as the 'Sahara of the Bozart' (writing the French words 'Beaux-Arts' as a Southerner would pronounce them), angry citizens of Atlanta retorted by saying, Coca-Cola was invented here, and that's a tremendous cultural achievement! Well, this is the place to inspect the 100-year-old cultural heritage of the brown beverage which has conquered the world! *Mon-Sat 9am-5pm, Sun 12pm-6pm; Admission: $6; 55 Martin Luther King Jr. Dr./Central Ave.; Tel: (404) 676-5151*

Eateries are located in the courtyards of malls and hotels. True Southern cuisine is rare. The international and multicultural styles dominate the kitchens of the larger cities.

Dining Room
As a cook in the Black Forest of Germany, chef Günter Seeger has earned two Michelin stars. Today he is the king of *haute cuisine* in Atlanta, offering innovative new dishes on the menu and excellent wines. *Reservations requested; Ritz-Carlton Buckhead Hotel, 3434 Peachtree Rd. NE; Tel: (404) 237-2700; Category 1*

Sierra Grill
The oysters, fahitas, fish and chili rellenos are as spicy as you would expect them to be in the Sierras of New Mexico. *1529 Piedmont Rd.; Tel: (404) 873-5360; Category 3*

103 West
If restaurant guides would award a star for kitsch, then this eatery would certainly earn one! Imitation marble figures and *trompe-l'oeil*. Good American and French cooking. *103 W Paces Ferry Rd.; Tel: (404) 233-5993; Category 2*

Lenox Square/Phipps Plaza
One of the largest and most frequented malls in the entire country. If you can find it in New York, you can find it here: Macy's, Saks, Tiffany and dozens of other boutiques and exclusive department stores. *Daily 9am-9pm, each store has its own opening hours; Peachtree/Lenox Rd.*

HOTELS

Crossroad Inn

Comfort at unbeatable prices, located 25 min. from downtown. Pool. *175 rooms; 4100 Wendell Dr. SW; Tel: (404) 696-0757; Fax: 696-5262; Category 3*

Omni

Pure science fiction: with a view of the CNN studios and the 15-storey high-tech scenery under the glass roof. Cozy? No! Interesting? Yes! *471 rooms; 100 CNN Center; Tel: (404) 659-0000; Fax: 818-4426; Category 1*

Westin Peachtree Plaza

Reserve a room on the 70th floor. No other hotel is located that high. Luxurious and friendly service despite the hotel's large size. Remarkable courtyards with waterfalls tumbling down eight floors. *1080 rooms; 210 Peachtree St.; Tel: (404) 659-1400; Fax: 589-759; Category 1*

ENTERTAINMENT

Despite the fact that Atlanta has been turned inside out, music clubs, soul and blues bars have surprisingly kept their hold on the city's nightlife.

Atlanta Nights, super-sized discotheque *(505 Peachtree St. NE; Tel: (404) 892-4998). Blues Harbor,* the name says it all *(155 Kenny's Alley; Tel: (404) 524-3001). Club Rio,* nightclub in a former film storage facility, the 'in' place to be *(195 Luckie St.; Tel: (404) 525-7467). Dante's Down the Hatch,* jazz and folk in Underground Atlanta *(Lower Alabama/Pryor St.; Tel: (404) 577-1800). Hemingway's,* the name is misleading, it's a country bar *(3910 N Druid Hills Rd.; Tel: (404) 325-3094). Walt Mitty's Jazz Café (816 N Highland Ave. NE; Tel: (404) 876-7115).*

INFORMATION

Convention & Visitors' Bureau

233 Peachtree St. NE, Suite 2000, Atlanta, GA 30303; Tel: (404) 222-6688

Visitor Information Center

From Mon-Fri 9am-6pm; Peachtree Center Mall; Lenox Square, 3394 Peachtree Rd. NE; Underground Atlanta, 65 Upper Alabama St.; Tel: (404) 222-6688, 521-6633 and 329-4500 (recording of current events)

CHARLESTON

(108/C6) This elegant city was founded in 1670 to honour Charles II. Its main purpose was to provide an export harbour for the products of the plantations: cotton, tobacco, rice and slaves. The Huguenots from France enriched Charleston's cultural heritage. Because of its many churches, Charleston was known as the 'Holy City'.

The elegant mansions of the prosperous farmers and merchants dominated the city's streets. During colonial times, Charleston grew to become the most important harbour on the Atlantic south of Philadelphia. During the Civil War, the residents of Charleston surrendered to the Union Army. After the city had been surrounded, they waited for some time but waved the white flag before the troops moved in. An earthquake in 1886 and 'Hurricane Hugo' in 1989

The elegance of Charleston in South Carolina

actually caused more damage to the city than the Civil War. Yet the majority of the 2,000 historical buildings remained relatively unscathed, allowing this area of four square miles to remain a true gem of the Old South.

SIGHTS

The Citadel
The military academy of the South, founded in 1842 on the site of a former fort that had been built to combat the uprisings of slaves. *Daily, Fri 3.45pm; military parade; Moultrie St./Elmwood Ave.; Tel: (843) 792-5006*

Fort Sumter
Impressive fort on an island in the Ashley River, where the first shots of the Civil War resounded on 12 April 1861. Boats depart from the City Marina on Lockwood Blvd. *Summer daily tours, 9.30am, 12 & 2.30pm; Admission: $10.50; Tel: (843) 722-1691*

Old Charleston
Explore the narrow cobblestone alleys on foot: Church, George and Meeting St.: *Nathaniel Russell House* with magnificent stairway *(51 Meeting St.); Edmondston-Alston House,* built in 1828 in a neoclassical style, a magnificent view of the harbour *(21 East Battery St.); Heyward-Washington House,* once the home of George Washington *(87 Church St.); Thomas Elfe Workshop,* studio of a famous carpenter *(54 Queen St.); Calhoun Mansion* with fabulous Victorian furnishings *(16 Meeting St.).*

INFORMATION

Visitor Information Center
For maps and tours. Many of the old buildings are open to the public. There are also films about the history of the city. *375 Meeting St.; Tel: (843) 853-8000*

RESTAURANTS

82 Queen
American cuisine, served in a historical building downtown. Nice courtyard. Specializing in fish. *82 Queen St.; Tel: (843) 723-7591; Category 2*

HOTELS

Heart of Charleston Quality Inn

In a historic area and furnished with antiques from the period. *126 rooms.; 125 Calhoun St.; Tel: (843) 722-3391; Fax: 577-0361; Category 2*

CHARLOTTESVILLE

(109/D2) This university, founded by Thomas Jefferson, has one of the most beautiful campuses in the USA. Arcades, red brick buildings, the gently sloping '-Lawn' and the serpentine-like walls combine to add to the harmonious atmosphere. This island of higher learning is crowned by the rotunda designed by Jefferson, who was inspired by the Pantheon in Rome, which he considered to be an example of perfect architecture. Monticello, the country mansion of the revolutionary war hero and president, is located outside Charlottesville.

SIGHTS

Monticello

A mixture of Palladian architecture and playfulness: Jefferson designed the exterior of his home according to the classical style of this Italian architect. The interior of the structure is filled with humourous surprises. In the foyer, for example, you'll find yourself standing upside down when you glance at your image in the mirror. Jefferson, a great statesman, was an original thinker: he used a double quill to write letters so that he could immediately have a copy of what he had written. And his position on the issue of slavery seems difficult to understand today. He called slavery a 'crime', yet himself kept slaves, whom he freed at his death. The remainders of 'Mulberry Row', the living quarters of 200 of Jefferson's slaves, are adjacent to his home. *Daily 8am-5pm; Admission: $8; 5 km (3.1 miles) south of Charlottesville on Highway 53*

University of Virginia

★ In 1976 the University of Virginia was officially named the greatest architectural masterpiece in the United States. The centre of the campus, the 'Lawn' between the Colonnades, is the best spot to get a complete view of the harmony of the campus. The rooms under the Colonnades have always been used as living quarters for students. One remains open for public viewing, Room No. 13. This was Edgar Allan Poe's room, the Dark Poet who was forced to leave the university in 1826. He was not able to pay tuition because he had lost his money gambling, and his father refused to send more. *Daily tours, 10 & 11am, 2, 3 & 4pm, free 45-min tours starting at the Rotunda; Tel: (804) 924-0311*

HOTELS

Boar's Head Inn

Colonial elegance. Tennis, golf. *173 rooms, US 250 west of the bypass US 29–250; Tel: (804) 296-2181; Fax: 977-1306; Category 1*

OUTER BANKS

(109/E4) The long, sand-dune islands off the coast of North Carolina, the Outer Banks, are one of the last few untouched natural landscapes on the East Coast of America: 150 km (94 miles) of sandy beaches, water fowl preserves in the salt marshes and the high dunes ★ of *Cape Hatteras* and picturesque old fishing villages such as Ocracoke or Kitty Hawk. Car ferries shuttle between the various islands.

MUSEUMS

Wright Brothers National Memorial

On 17 December 1903, Orville Wright completed the first motorized flight. It lasted 12 seconds. The museum houses a replica of the first airplane and many other airplane models. *Near Kitty Hawk; Daily 9am-5pm, summer until 7pm; Admission: $1*

RICHMOND

(**109/D2**) During the Civil War, the state capital of Virginia was named the 'capital of the Confederacy'. The *Museum of the Confederacy* provides an overview of the time of the war between the states. Today, Richmond (pop. 200,000) is a banking centre and still prominent in the processing of tobacco.

SAVANNAH

(**108/B6**) ★ The sleepy South, unbelievable heat: the books of history had positive and negative things in store for this city on Georgia's coast. In 1733, Savannah was planned as the first modern settlement in the British colonies of North America. In 1864, General Sherman of the North decided to spare this important harbour for cotton trade, leaving it untouched during his 'March to the Sea'. After that, Savannah deteriorated — the plantations experienced their downfall since they were no longer profitable without the use of slaves. Local residents didn't begin restoring Savannah to its former glory until the '50s. A walk through the city under the shade of the oak trees, which are covered with Spanish moss, takes you back in time to the heart of the Old South. The Historic District is in the centre of town, where streets are arranged in a grid format.

One of the traditional mansions, the *Owens-Thomas House,* which dates to the colonial times, can be toured *(Tue-Sat 10am-5pm; Sun and Mon 2-5pm; Admission: $5; 124 Abercorn St.).* The *History Museum* is located in the train station of the Central of Georgia Railroad *(daily 8.30am-5pm; Admission $3; 303 Martin Luther King Jr. Blvd.),* and Savannah even has a small but recommendable *Black Heritage Museum (Mon-Fri 12-4pm, Sat and Sun 2 pm-4.30pm; Admission: $1.75; King Tisdell Cottage. 514 E Huntingdon St.).* The Black Heritage Museum provides a very educational way of discovering the history of Savannah and its Afro-American population – you provide the car and the museum provides the guide at a cost of $6.

HOTELS

The Mulberry

This hotel is located in the centre of town in a former horse stall which later housed a Coca-Cola bottling facility. The building has been carefully restored and includes many antique furnishings. The hotel also has a nice courtyard. *148 rooms, 601 E Bay St.; Tel: (912) 238-1200; Fax: 236-2184; Category 2*

Edgar Allan Poe was a student at the University of Virginia in Charlottesville

WILLIAMSBURG

(109/E2) Williamsburg, which served as capital of Virginia during the colonial era, is located near Richmond, the current capital of Virginia and former capital of the Confederate States. The entire town is one large museum, and the most famous museum city within the USA. Former president Ronald Reagan once held the world economic summit here – Williamsburg offered the best photo setting this close to Washington, D. C. The more than one million annual tourists must feel the same way. In the 150 buildings of the site, virtually everything has remained just as it was in the time between 1698 and 1780. Craftsmen demonstrate their trades, bakers bake bread like back then and the women are dressed in the clothing of the era. The *capitol* and the *governor's mansion tower above all other buildings.* Jefferson, Henry and other revolutionary figures debated their plans to overthrow British rule in the *Raleigh Tavern.*

Anyone who was caught by the spies who were loyal to the British crown had to spend time in the *Public Gaol. East of Richmond on Colonial Parkway; Daily 8.30am-8pm, winter 8.30am-5pm; Admission: $33; Tel: (800) 447-8679*

INFORMATIONS

Williamsburg Visitor Center
Information, maps, tickets, hotel reservations. *Colonial Parkway/Hwy. 132; Tel: (757) 253-0192*

SURROUNDING AREA

Jamestown Settlement
(109/E2) The reconstruction of the first settlement on the East Coast that Europeans founded at the mouth of the James River in 1607. An Indian village and the ships that carried the settlers from Europe can also be toured. The outstanding *Museum on the History of Settlement* is especially interesting. *Daily 9am-5pm; Admission: $9.75; Tel: (757) 229-1607*

Vacation time all year round

This recreational paradise is at everyone's doorstep – for Europeans as well

The southernmost tip of the South – the subtropical peninsula on the Tropic of Cancer – is best described as having a 13,550-km (8,470-mile) long coastline. Some more statistics: The average temperature in January is 24.4 °C (76°F); the number of rainy days per year, five. These statistics apply to Miami and are, of course, averages, but they explain why the southern half of the Florida peninsula is the number one holiday destination in America. *Have fun in Florida!* This message appears everywhere, and resounds from all sides. Despite the greatly increasing number of European tourists, the definition of *fun* remains American, meaning: *fun* as in not just plain old fun, but a more active way of enjoying life.

Three major aspects make Florida worth the trip: beautiful tropical beaches reminiscent of the South Sea, a modern infrastructure that is usually present in tropical areas and the seemingly perfect entertainment industry.

Before the house, the car;
behind the house, the motorboat:
Fort Lauderdale

What are you looking for? Sports activities? Golf, tennis, deep-sea fishing, snorkelling, diving, surfing, sailing? And for more passive sports enthusiasts: horse racing, polo, car racing, Jai-Alai – just ask the clerk at the hotel reception. Looking for deserted beaches? Take a short drive away from the major beaches and you'll find one. Beaches where the favourite pastime is *people watching*, where volleyball matches occur spontaneously and lead to new friendships? Try the lively beaches of any coastal town. Nightlife? In countless bars, discotheques and other entertainment spots, night becomes day.

Between the coasts, you'll find: the unique swampland of the Everglades, citrus orchards, Orlando's Disney World and a dozen other amusement parks, cattle and horse farms and, finally, wooded areas, lakes and rivers where hunters and canoe paddlers abound. The Kennedy Space Center, where the space shuttles are assembled and launched, gives tourists the impression that there is something else to do in Florida beyond spending holidays and retirement under the sun. But that impression is deceiving. The space centre is an exception. In general, the entire local population of Florida thrives on the fact that others are having fun here.

CAPE CANAVERAL

(**112/C3**) The John F. Kennedy Space Center has been used as a rocket testing facility since 1949. In 1958 it became the launching site for space missions of the United States. As part of the tour, you'll see the Vehicle Assembly Building, which is 160-m (520-ft) tall. Clouds sometimes form inside because of the height of the building. You'll also see the space travel museum, the Cape Kennedy Air Force Station, the actual launching facilities, the astronaut training centre and the control centre. Bus tours commence at the Visitors' Center. *Daily 9am-8pm (except during launches), Red Tour (more interesting, includes visit to the training centre) and Blue Tour (incl. Imax Cinema), each tour $19; Tel: (407) 452-2121*

KEY WEST

(**112/C6**) ★ The last of the islands comprising the chain of the 'Florida Keys' at the state's southernmost tip is the most beautiful. It's also a favourite gathering for eccentric people and homosexuals. A five-hour drive from Miami via the Overseas Highway brings tourists to the island with an area of nearly ten square kilometres (6 sq miles). After Hawaii, Key West is the second most southern point of the United States. Ernest Hemingway lived and worked here and wrote his tall tales under

the influence of many drinks. Beautiful conch homes line the streets, built by sailors who modelled their dwellings after various things they'd seen around the world. There aren't many beaches here. Instead, lots of entertainment. Many bars maintain to be 'Hemingway's favourite'; extensive Mardi Gras celebrations are held in the spring. On Mallory Pier, you'll find live street entertainment with jugglers and musicians.

SIGHTS

Ernest Hemingway Home and Museum
The author's home was built in 1851 in a Spanish colonial style. Hemingway worked in an adjoining building that was off limits to the children. *Daily 9am-5pm; Admission: $6.50; 907 Whitehead St.; Tel: (305) 294-1575*

ENTERTAINMENT

Captain Tony's Saloon (428 Green St.) and *Sloppy Joe's (201 Duval St.)* compete for the honour of being 'Hemingway's favourite bar'. After a few of the author's favourite drinks, daiquiries and margaritas, you may no longer know in which of the two bars you're sitting. And you probably won't care either.

MIAMI

(**113/D5**) Aside from its location, Florida's glittering metropolis has as little to do with the southern states as Copenhagen has to do with the Alps. But let's exaggerate a bit. When the sun sinks over the Everglades, the colour of the

MARCO POLO SELECTION: FLORIDA

1 Art Deco District
The fashionable quarter of Miami Beach, all in pink and other pastel colours (page 67)

2 Everglades
Swamps, alligators and the world of birds (page 70)

3 Drive to Key West
170 km (106 mi) with 42 bridges over the ocean (page 66)

4 'Back to the Future'
The wildest ride among all of the Orlando amusement parks (page 70)

sky is transformed into purple, and the last rays of sun reflect in the glass panes of the postmodern skyscrapers, Miami awakens for the second time each day – for the nightlife.

Fashion models are applying fresh make-up in their rooms in the Art Deco hotels of Miami Beach. (After all, it seems like this is the only site for fashion shoots.) More mature women are hustling to the beauty parlours in the hotels. The waiters of the Cuban restaurants are posting the daily specials of *tapas y mariscos,* Spanish snacks and shellfish. Male customers at the neon bars are stirring their frozen margaritas as their eyes lay in wait for the *jeunesse dorée.* And preparations are going on in the nightclubs. The strippers are trying on their brassieres and the thin garders whose sole purpose is to collect the dollar bills they're paid by their voyeuristic fans.

Miami is the hottest city in the United States, both literally and figuratively. Adding to this reputation is the increase of crime in recent years. That in turn has led to improved security measures.

SIGHTS

Art Deco District of Miami Beach

★ Shades of pink and other pastels, the ocean liner portholes and the wavy decorations above the windows, the delicate colours and nautical patterns of the buildings throughout the southern part of Miami Beach are enchanting. Not long ago, the largest collection of Art Deco buildings in the world, built in the '20s and '30s, would have been condemned to the wrecking ball. The passing of time and the salt-filled air had deteriorated the colourful façades. The only tourists sunning themselves on the aluminium chairs outside the hotels were the elderly – thrifty retirees. Investors decided to create a brand new Miami Beach by tearing down buildings and starting over. But a group of citizens opposed their plans. The district, which includes 40 city blocks, was added to the National Register of Historic Places.

Tours, lasting approximately ninety minutes, are offered by the Miami Design Preservation League: *Thurs 6.30pm, Sat 10.30am; Admission: $10; starting at the Welcome Center; 1001 Ocean Dr.; Tel: (305) 672-2014*

*One of the 'skyscrapers'
in the Art Deco district of
Miami Beach*

Bayside Marketplace

If we apply the criteria we have chosen to categorize various places, then we would not classify the Bayside Marketplace under 'sightseeing', but under 'shopping'. But we do have a sociological argument prepared to justify our decision. Shopping is a major component of the American way of life, and Bayside is the incarnation of the place to go shopping. It's not a typical mall consisting of a large cement box-like construction which has a wonderful ambience on the inside. Instead, the 'Marketplace' is made up of two gracefully arched, open pavilions at the yacht harbour.

The planners of this facility tried to create a classical market which is actually reminiscent of an oriental bazaar. Rather than just housing boutiques and de-

partment stores, the owners of the small sales booths and snack bars, representing nearly every nationality, have been encouraged to transform the Bayside Marketplace into a true marketplace. Jugglers and magicians, parrot keepers and music groups often provide live entertainment. *Mon-Sat 10am-10pm, Sun 12 noon-8pm; 401 Biscayne Blvd.*

Downtown Miami

Space was rare in downtown Miami, but not money. From dubious sources of income which - needed to be laundered. So, what could be done with it? The Answer: give the downtown area a facelift by erecting taller buildings, designed by the best architects. Reflecting glass and the unusually coloured façades tend to hide the fact that at least a third of the offices in these postmodern skyscrapers are standing vacant. And another achievement of modern technology is hardly utilized: the Metro Mover — a high-tech overhead railway with large windows.

The Metro Mover route takes the form of a ring around the downtown area, providing an ideal sightseeing tour at practically no cost: one ticket costs 25 cents.

Vizcaya

Let's take a trip into the past, into the year 1916: James Deering had a barn full of money because he'd made lots of money in agriculture. His company International Harvester produced agricultural machinery and had been so profitable that he could afford to build a villa in southern Miami. He spent an astronomical amount of money on a dream villa, which combined various architectural styles: a bit of rococo, a dash of baroque, a splash of renaissance and a breath of neoclassicism. Rigidly organized gardens were planted, and the 70 rooms of the eclectic palace on Biscayne Bay filled with art treasures. Deering even had some money left, so he had a boat launch made of stone erected just off his private coast. This turned out to be an investment for the future. During the prohibition, mysterious ships were seen anchored there. Although this assertion was never proved, it certainly seems plausible: the ships are rumoured to have carried illegal hard liquor. *Daily 9.30am-5pm; Admission: $8; 3251 S Miami Ave.; Tel: (305) 579-2708*

RESTAURANTS

Café Chauveron

Fantastic French cuisine: salmon mousse with lobster sauce, chateaubriand etc. *Closed from June to Oct; 9561 E Bay Harbor Dr.; Tel: (305) 866-8779; Category 1*

Joe's Seafood Market

Fantastic American seafood: shrimp, lobster, perch, angelfish at unbelievably low prices. *400 NW North River Dr. (diffiicult to find because it's located directly on a pier: from Biscayne Blvd. turn west onto NW 3rd St., and then right at North River Dr.); Tel: (305) 374-5637; Category 2*

Versailles

Cubans eat here. The mirrors are as ornate as the reflecting glass in the real Versailles outside Paris. The medianoche sandwiches are the most impressive. Cuban cuisine in Little Havana. *3555 SW 8th St.; Tel: (305) 445-7614; Category 2*

HOTELS

Cardozo

This building located directly on Miami Beach is the finest example of Art Deco restoration, providing the most accurate example of that period. However, not all the rooms have original Art Deco furnishings. If you want the best, then request: *A renovated ocean-view room, please. 45 rooms; 4 suites; 1144 Ocean Dr.; Tel: (305) 535-6500; no fax; Category 1; 30% reduced rate in the summer*

Fontainebleau Hilton Resort and Spa

Typical design of the Hilton chain but one of the best versions: huge pool with tropical scenery, direct on the beach, sports facilities, beauty care, elegant restaurants. *1,206 rooms, 60 suites; 4441 Collins Ave.; Tel: (305) 538-2000; Fax: 531-9274; Category 1; 25% reduced rate in the summer*

ENTERTAINMENT

Cactus Cantina Grill

Live music: blues, rockabilly, soul. *Daily 5pm-5am; cover charge for special events; Miami Beach, 630 6th St.; Tel: (305) 532-5095*

Club Tropigala

High energy revue – in the United States that stands for long-legged dancers. *Wed, Thurs, Sun at 8.30pm, Fri and Sat at 8 and 10 pm; Admission: $13.50, for dinner show $44; 4441 Collins Ave., in Hilton Hotel; Tel: (305) 538-2000*

Les Violins

A mixture of carnival in Rio and a Broadway musical. *Daily 9 and 11pm; Admission: $10, with dinner $39; 1751 Biscayne Blvd.; Tel: (305) 371-9910*

Penrod's on the Beach

⚓ Discotheque and singles' bar with beach and pool. *Sun-Thurs 11pm-2am, Fri and Sat 11pm-5am; Admission: $18 for people under 21, $5 for 21 & older; Miami Beach, Ocean Dr./1st St.; Tel: (305) 538-1111*

INFORMATION

Greater Miami Convention and Visitors' Bureau

Mon-Fri 8.30am-5pm; Miami, 701 Brickell Ave., Suite 2700; Tel: (305) 539-3063

SURROUNDING AREA

Everglades   (112/C5–6)

★ This subtropical swamp, North America's largest marshy area, abounds in rare plants and animals. Located southwest of the Miami limits. In 1992, hurricane 'Andrew' destroyed the visitors' centre near Homestead and the wooden walkways that lead throughout the wildlife preserve. Most of the pathways in this unique biotope have been reconstructed.

ORLANDO

(112/C3) The home of Mickey Mouse. Without Walt Disney, Orlando would be a sleepy town in central Florida. Thanks to the biggest of the Disney amusement parks with the greatest number of visitors each year, and to the doz-

ens of other amusement parks in the area, Orlando has become a fast-growing, affluent city full of variety. Universal Studios allowed the master of illusion, Steven Spielberg, to develop a facility to compete with Disney's MGM Studios. Shamu, the killer whale weighing in at 4,400 lbs, gives his pretty trainer a kiss. Wet'n'Wild is Orlando's solution to the lack of coastline — providing water fun without a beach: 'Kamikaze' water slides and the 'Surf' pool with waves up to seven feet high. In castles from the 'Middle Ages' made of paper maché, you can pretend to dine with Henry VIII or spend time in the torture chamber — it's difficult to see where Orlando begins and ends. It seems as if the entire Orlando area is one big animated movie.

SIGHTS

Universal Studios Florida

Here you can become part of the action of such popular films as *King Kong, E. T. or* ★ *Back to the Future.* You'll experience 8.3 points on the Richter scale on the Earthquake Ride. You can take a stroll on Hollywood's Sunset Boulevard, in New York's Central Park or on San Francisco's Ghirardelli Square — what more could you desire? *Daily 9am-7pm, on weekends and until 10pm in the summer; Admission: adults $37, children age 3-9 $30, under 3 free; near the interchange connecting I-4 and the Florida Turnpike; 1000 Universal Studios Plaza; Tel: (407) 363-8000*

Walt Disney World

Looking for more? Then make *Disney MGM Studios* your next

trip with *Aliens, Indiana Jones* and Grauman's Chinese Theater, which only comprise a small part of Disney World. The *Magic Kingdom* with Cinderella's castle and Main Street USA is the classic part, similar to the Disney theme parks in Los Angeles and Paris. The *Epcot Center* (Experimental Prototype Community of Tomorrow) shows you how the world of tomorrow was imagined 20 years ago. We can compare our current world with how it was envisioned. Beyond the three main parks, there is more: the water and adventure worlds called *Discovery Island, River Country* and *Typhoon Lagoon.* It's impossible to visit more than one park per day. The Magic Kingdom is so popular that waiting for more than an hour for certain attractions is normal. So bring plenty of patience. *Daily 9am to at least 8pm, usually until 11pm or midnight; day pass for one park: adults $38.10, Children age 3-9 $30.60, under 3 free, 4-Day-Pass for all three theme parks: $141.55 and $113.05, 5-Day-Pass for the theme parks plus Pleasure Island, Typhoon Lagoon, River Country and Discovery Island: $189.15 and $151.10; entrance via Interstate 4 and Irlo Bronson Memorial Highway (192/530), you won't miss the signs guiding you to the various sites; Tel: (407) 824-8000 (to order tickets), (407) 824-4321 (Information), (407) 824-4500 (Guest Relations – general assistance)*

HOTELS

With everything organized perfectly in the theme parks, how could it be different with accommodation? Hotels of varying price categories are located in Disney World. Some are accessible via the railway that leads through the parks. There is also a great camping site. *Tel: (407) 934-7639*

ST. PETERSBURG/ TAMPA

(112/B4) These cities lie along Tampa Bay, which is known as the 'retiree's paradise'. St. Petersburg and Tampa are close to the tropical beaches of the warm Gulf of Mexico. Tampa's *Ybor City,* once a major cigar manufacturing facility and now a kind of living museum, is where Cuban national hero José Martí, a reader in a cigar factory, wrote the lyrics to the song 'Guantanamera'. The twin cities are a good starting point for an excursion to the islands of Sanibel and Captiva, which seem to have been taken directly from a Gauguin painting. Or visit Tarpon Springs, the town founded by Greek immigrants who made their living by harvesting sponges in the surrounding waters.

HOTELS

Don CeSar

A veritable pink palace that was nearly demolished but is now a national landmark and thus protected. Affluent hotel guests can enjoy its luxurious ambiance. *277 rooms; 3400 Gulf Blvd., St. Petersburg; Tel: 813 360-1881; Fax: 367-3609; Category 1*

More detailed information on Florida can be found in the MARCO POLO guide *Florida.*

Slow water, hot jazz

On the trail of Huckleberry Finn

O*l' man river, he just keeps rolling along.* How many times have songs been written and sung as a tribute to the great Mississippi? Muddy brown waters roll slowly along her banks, at least on the last leg of its 2,962-km (185-mile) journey to the South. The third-longest river in the world has humble beginnings, not much more than a brook at Itsaca Lake in northwestern Minnesota. There the water is a clear blue, and cold — much more romantic than on the stretches down South where Huckleberry Finn and the runaway slave Jim cross the Mississippi in Mark Twain's novel.

The first, gentle section of the Mississippi, which extends to St. Anthony Falls near Minneapolis measures 842 km (526 miles) in length. Together, St. Paul, on the eastern shore, and Minneapolis form 'The Twin Cities'. Minneapolis is known as the livelier and more successful of the two. Both cities are agricultural cen-

New Orleans: musicians' from all over the world come here to enjoy the music

tres. Located here among the huge wheat fields are the headquarters of giants of the American food industry: General Mills and Pillsbury, and the Grain Exchange, the largest grain market in the country. Both cities are clean and orderly. Wintertime, the most memorable aspect of the Twin Cities, brings bitter cold and record-breaking temperatures every year.

Ten American states border on the Mississippi River: on the eastern side are Wisconsin, Illinois, Tennessee and Mississippi. Despite the immense size of the remaining stretch of the river, the only other cities we have chosen to mention are St. Louis, Memphis and New Orleans.

It's difficult to imagine travel on the slow-paced paddle-wheel steamboats of the Mississippi River — we can only guess how long it took to get from one place to the next. If you want to truly get a feel for the journeys of the last century, take a trip on the river in one of the colourful paddle-wheel steamers. Boat rides of varying lengths originate in the major cities along the river. The most beautiful round-trip boat ride is the line running from Dubuque to Davenport in Iowa, because the river still has a nice blue hue up north. However, after the Wisconsin, the Ohio, the Missouri and the Arkansas rivers have emptied their waters into the Mississippi so that it swells to a formidable size, it's very easy to see why people here call the great river 'Old Muddy'.

Artefacts continue to draw countless fans to Elvis Presley's home Graceland near Memphis

(**110/C1**) Memphis is known for its paddle-wheel steamers on the Mississippi and for Elvis Presley – who made his claim to fame here. Yet Memphis is the largest city in Tennessee (pop. 670,000) and simultaneously the 18th largest city in the USA. It is a modern and an affluent major city with the world's largest cotton market and a prominent river harbour. The sound of Blues and Rock'n'Roll seems to hang in the air. So: *Put on your blue suede shoes.*

SIGHTS

Graceland

★ Never heard of it? Then forget it. Can you hear it? Then hurry up and go to Elvis Presley's southern mansion. Elvis's stage costumes: unbelievably ornate! His grave: tear-evoking. In 1954, a music manager named Sam Phillips exclaimed, 'If only I could find a white boy who can sing like a black boy – then I'd be a millionaire'. Phillips found what he was looking for in Elvis

MARCO POLO SELECTION: THE MISSISSIPPI VALLEY

1 Absinthe Bar
Lively bar where Jazz and Blues dictate the rhythm (page 78)

2 Graceland
Pilgrimage site and a definite must for all Elvis Presley fans (page 74)

3 Hannibal
The classic story *The Adventures of Tom Sawyer* was set here (page 79)

4 Nashville
The Grand Ol' Opry is the heart of the Country & Western world (page 76)

Presley, sold him for $35,000. But Phillips did manage to make his million with other singers ,such as Carl Perkins and Jerry Lee Lewis. Yet Presley was even more successful. At Graceland you can see an extensive exhibit of all the tacky objects he purchased with his money. You'll also be amazed by the devotion of the fans who continue to adore the King of Rock'n'Roll. He remains a myth. *Daily 8am-6pm, winter 9am-6pm; Admission: $10 (mansion only), $18.50 (mansion, airplanes, museum and the singer's tour bus); 3717 Elvis Presley Blvd.; Tel: (901) 332-3322 (reservations mandatory!)*

HOTELS

The Peabody
Standing out next to the Holiday Inns, Omni and Marriott hotels is the Peabody, the *grande dame* from 1925, renovated in the neo-Renaissance style. The real live ducks are one surprising feature of the Peabody. Each morning they waddle from their penthouse on the roof to the marble fountain in the foyer. *454 rooms; 149 Union Ave.; Tel: (901) 529-4000; Fax: 529-3600; Category 1*

RESTAURANTS

Leonard's
Memphis claims to be the *pork barbecue capital of the world,* the world capital of grilled ribs. Leonard's is the favourite of the nearly one hundred restaurants, a real institution in Memphis. If you don't want to gnaw on the bones, order Outside Brown, chopped pork grilled to a crispy brown. *Opening times vary; 1140 Bellevue Blvd. South; Tel: (901) 948-1581; Category 3*

ENTERTAINMENT

The times of Elvis are irrevocably over, as are the times of Johnny Ace and Bobby Bland. But for the benefit of the tourists, they continue in an artificial form at Beale St. and on Overton Square.

B. B. King's Blues Club
Opened in 1991. Blues seven evenings a week. Sometimes BB himself performs. *147 Beale St.; Tel: (901) 527-5464*

Orpheum Theatre
Broadway shows, operas, classic movies in a beautifully restored theatre. *203 Main St.; Tel: (901) 525-3000*

MINNEAPOLIS/ ST. PAUL

(**100/A4**) The Twin Cities on both sides of the Mississippi River have a combined total population of 2.5 million people. St. Paul, the smaller and older of the two, was founded as a fur trading post on the north bank of the river in 1840. St. Paul is also Minnesota's state capital. You can't miss the old part of the city with the State Capitol building and the St. Paul Cathedral, a replica of St. Peter's Cathedral in Rome. The skyscrapers of Minneapolis on the other side of the river, the economically strong, more modern half of the Twin Cities. The best view of downtown is from the Nicollet Mall, a busy pedestrian area between the Mississippi and beautiful Loring Park.

MUSEUMS

Fort Snelling
This restored military post built in 1825 is now an open-air museum. *1 May–30 Sep daily 10am-5pm; Admission: $4; on the riverbank near the intersection of Highways 5 and 55; Tel: (612) 725-2413*

Walker Art Center
Modern art and wonderful, sculptured gardens. *Tues-Sat 10am-5pm, Sun 11am-5pm, gardens 6am-midnight; Admission: $4; 725 Vineland Place; Tel: (612) 375-7600*

INFORMATION

Minnesota Office of Tourism
375 Jackson St., St. Paul, MN 55101; Tel: (612) 296-5029

NASHVILLE

(**107/E5**) ★ Located in the mountains of Tennessee is another one of the 'music cities'. Like Memphis, Nashville is a modern metropolis, full of highways. Nashville is known as the 'Athens of the South' because it features numerous neoclassical, colonial and Victorian structures, and of course it is famous as 'Music City USA', at least for Country & Western music. But Nashville can also be classified as the new capital of the American automobile and insurance industries.

SIGHTS

Opryland USA
A sort of Disney World of music: a show park with 21 musical carousel rides, 12 stages, wandering singers, bands and clowns. *Opening hours vary, so it's better to ring*

ahead of time; One-day pass: $28.99; Briley Parkway; Tel: (615) 889-6700

NEW ORLEANS

(**118/C5**) A sign hanging on the door of the Old Absinthe House is flattering to the women and attracts the men at the same time: 'The most beautiful women in the world walk through these doors'. The Absinthe House, built in 1826, is the only establishment in Vieux Carré, also known as the French Quarter, which was able to avoid the commercialization of everything that once mattered in New Orleans. In this place, known as 'The Cradle of Jazz', that's exactly what is played. The cuisine is Creole: spicy, fatty and complemented by lots of rice and beans, the way the Spanish-French residents liked it. Mardi Gras is carnival, enhanced by African mysticism and Latin-American rhythms. In the French Quarter, Dixieland bands play pop music, and the Blues resounds from the bayous.

SIGHTS

French Quarter
The heart of New Orleans is best seen by walking without a specific destination. Wrought-iron balcony railings, walls with ornate plasterwork, tall brick walls and courtyards provide enough orientation: where you stop seeing these characteristics is where the French Quarter stops. Looking for tarot card readers? Look between Canal Street and Esplanade Avenue, between the Louis Armstrong Park and the Mississippi.

Jackson Square, known for its Spanish colonial-style architecture from the end of the 18th century, is located in the middle of the quarter. The original French architecture was destroyed during the great fires of 1788 and 1794. The *St. Louis Cathedral* is also located here. This is the third structure on this site, to which the Catholics of this most Catholic city of North America flock. The adjacent buildings with the magnificent balcony is the Cabildo, one-time headquarters of the Spanish government. In St. Peter and St. Ann streets, you'll find the *Pontalba Buildings,* remarkable apartment and office buildings built in 1850; House No. 523 on St. Ann Street, which belongs to a member of the Creole upper class, is open to the public *(Wed-Sun 10am -5pm; Admission: $3).*

From *Moon Walk,* a wooden promenade on the other side of Decatur St., you have a good view of the harbour. At the *French Market,* dating from 1720, all kinds of objects are now sold. But you'll find more interesting things being sold each weekend at the *Farmer's Market,* located downriver. During the week, fruit and vegetables are sold there around the clock.

Esplanade Avenue is lined with oak trees and large Creole villas. At the beginning of the street is the *Old US Mint,* now home to the *Jazz Museum,* which features exhibits on music history as well as on Mardi Gras, and displays the original street car named 'Desire', built in 1906 *(Wed-Sun 10am-5pm; Admission: $3).*

From Esplanade Avenue turn left onto *Bourbon Street,* the pedestrian mall and former main street of amusement, a boulevard full of souvenir shops, cafés, topless bars and restaurants.

MUSEUMS

The Historic Voodoo Museum
Have you ever wanted to torture someone by sticking needles in a doll looking like him? Did you ever want to know why white slave drivers were afraid of their wives performing ritual dances in front of black men without their clothes? This is the place to find out. *Daily 10am-7pm; Admission: $5; 724 Dumaine; Tel: (504) 523-7685*

RESTAURANTS

Acme Oyster House
Oysters are served here on a marble bar. Favourite stop for police officers, and they ought to know where the food is best.
724 Iberville St.; Tel: (504) 522-5973; Category 3

Café du Monde
Beignets and café au lait. Very, very popular. *800 Decatur St.; Tel: (504) 581-2914; Category 2*

K-Paul's Louisiana Kitchen
No reservations; be prepared to wait at the door. For what? The most authentic Cajun fish cuisine in the entire French Quarter.
416 Chartres St.; Tel: (504) 524-7394; Category 1

HOTELS

Bourbon New Orleans
Historical hotel — canopy beds are nearly mandatory here — swimming pool and pleasant service. *167 rooms; 47 suites; 717 Orleans St.; Tel: (504) 523-2222; Fax: 571-4666; Category 1*

French Quarter Maisonettes

Quiet Bed & Breakfast with nice courtyard. Make reservations in advance! *7 rooms; 1130 Chartres St.; Tel/Fax: (504) 524-9918; Category 2–3*

Prytania Park

Sixty-two rooms and very charming; 13 rooms in a restored Victorian townhouse, located on the premises. *1519 Terpsichore St.; Tel: (504) 524-0427; Fax: 522-2977; Category 1–2*

Villa Convento

Simple Bed & Breakfast in an old Creole townhouse. *24 rooms; 616 Ursulines St.; Tel: (504) 522-1793; Fax: 524-1902; Category 2*

ENTERTAINMENT

During Mardi Gras (French: fat Tuesday), which runs the two weeks before the time of fasting (Lent) begins, New Orleans is one big party. Special events include the presence of Zula, an Afro-American who parodies the Carnival Prince; the hooded and torch-bearing men of the nightly Comus Parade, which is said to have racist undertones; and fancy homosexual balls at which heterosexuals are parodied and the most daring costumes can be found.

The following establishments are recommended year-round:

Absinthe Bar

★ A small, dark bar with an original feeling. Lots of jazz as well as rhythm and blues. *Open daily; Fri and Sat minor cover charge; 400 Bourbon St.; Tel: (504) 525-8108*

New Storyville Jazz Hall

Dixieland music for the entire family. *Every evening; prices vary; 1104 Decatur St.; Tel: (504) 522-2500*

Petroleum Lounge

Truly regional brass music (trumpets and horns). *Hours vary, 1st drink $3; 1501 St. Philip St.; Tel: (504) 523-0248*

Preservation Hall

No beverages, no chairs, in poor condition and still the place to go to see grand old jazz musicians perform. *Daily, best after midnight; 726 St. Peter St.; Tel: (504) 522-2841 (daytime), 523-8939 (evening)*

INFORMATION

Greater New Orleans Tourist & Convention Commission
Mon-Fri 9am-6pm, 1520 Sugar Bowl Dr., New Orleans, LA 70112; Tel: (504) 566-5031; Fax: 566-5046

ST. LOUIS

(106/C3) In 1850, the city near the fork of the Missouri and Mississippi rivers was the 'Gate to the West' for hundreds of thousands of pioneers. St. Louis became one of the most important industrial areas in America in the 20th century; revenues are generated by breweries and the automobile and airplane industries. With a population of 2.5 million people, St. Louis is the largest city in the Mississippi Valley.

SIGHTS

During the '80s, St. Louis carefully restored the deteriorating downtown area along Market

Street to its former glory. Boutiques and restaurants have moved into the old storage buildings of the Laclede's Landing historical quarter.

West of downtown you'll find *Forest Park,* the nearly 500-ha (1,235-acre) large section of town. The *St. Louis Art Museum* is located in the only remaining building from the 1904 World's Fair (numerous paintings by German expressionists).

Gateway Arch

✎ The 192-m (624-ft) tall steel arch on the banks of the Mississippi is the landmark of St. Louis. It was erected in 1965 as a monument to the westward migration of the American pioneers. Museum at the base of the arch. *Daily 8am-10pm, winter to 6pm; Admission: $1, elevator $2.50; Riverfront Park; Tel: (314) 982-1410*

SHOPPING

Union Station

The impressive train station from 1894 on the corner of Market St. and 18th St. has been renovated to become a shopping centre.

HOTELS

Hyatt Regency Union Station

540 luxury class rooms in an old train station. *1 St. Louis Union Station; Tel: (314) 231-1234; Fax: 923-3970; Category 1*

Regal Riverfront

Good middle-class hotel near the riverfront with ✎ rotating restaurant on the top floor. *853 rooms; 200 South 4th St.; Tel: (314) 241-9500; Fax: 241-9601; Category 2*

SURROUNDING AREA

Hannibal   (106/B2)

★ Novelist Mark Twain spent his childhood in this small town about two hours northwest of St. Louis.

Several sights, including the *Mark Twain Caverns,* will bring 'The Adventures of Tom Sawyer' to life for the visitor.

Meramec Caverns   (106/B3)

Large stalactite caverns, which are definitely worth the trip, are located approximately 100 km (63 miles) southwest of St. Louis, near *Stanton.*

Just like it used to be! Paddle-wheel steamers on the Mississippi

Structural changes on the Great Lakes

An adaptable economy fights decreasing
population and stagnating trade

Buffalo, located in the state of New York, was the historical starting point for the settlement of the Midwest. Through the end of the 19th century, Buffalo remained the harbour where goods were transferred from the industrial cities to the Great Lakes. Today, the Erie Canal which ends in Buffalo is no longer being utilized, and the city has long since ceased being the gate to the rest of America. But it is still a good starting point for tourists to forge their way into the Great Lakes region — especially since the fundamental transformation the region has experienced during the 20th century is so evident here.

The cities along the canal, which extends through all of New York up to Albany on the Hudson River, are no longer as prosperous as they once were. The canal was opened in 1825, enabling a flourishing shipping industry from Lake Superior to New York City at the mouth of the Hudson River. Things are much quieter here now, but some warehouses, factories and a

The John Hancock Center, Chicago

number of magnificent mansions testify to the time when the Erie Canal was a sort of aorta leading from the industrial heart of the country to the lakes.

The southern shore of Lake Erie takes you through a small corner of New York and Pennsylvania, before reaching the other states bordering the Great Lakes: Ohio, Indiana, Illinois, Michigan, Wisconsin and Minnesota.

En route to Detroit in the north, you'll be surprised to discover a wine region in northern Ohio. The winegrowers produce decent results that you can test for yourself. Much of the grapes are transformed into grape jelly, the second ingredient for the famous peanut butter and jelly sandwich, found in lunch pails across the country.

You'll pass through the classic industrial cities of Cleveland and Toledo along Lake Erie, which bear the marks of their past glory and the difficulties of adjusting to the downfall of the industrial age. However, you'll be surprised to discover the beautiful sandy beaches along the second smallest of the Great Lakes, which give the impression of a large sea.

Of course, Detroit (situated between Lake Erie and Lake Huron and a stone's throw away from Canada) and Chicago remain the symbols of the Great Lakes.

There's one thing you should remember: an average American adult drives about 12,000 km (7,500 miles) each year. This great mobility began in Detroit. The automobile was not invented in Detroit, and the first American-made automobile was not assembled there. But it's where Henry Ford began construction of his car for the average person in 1893. Soon thereafter, mass production of his Ford Model T began to make history. In 1919, one million cars were completed on the assembly lines which helped mould history.

Chicago's claim to fame went hand in hand with the industrialization of agriculture. Contrary to the romanticized view of th+ world of cowboys, the slaughterhouses of the windy city not only processed cattle from Texas, but primarily swine, which was delivered there by rail to what was once the largest freight station in the world. As a result, an unpleasant odour permeated Chicago. The most prominent slaughter-houses were closed in 1971. The reduction of that industry occurred nearly parallel with the first attempts of Japanese automakers to penetrate the American market. Today, since one in three cars driven in the United States is Japanese-made, both cities show clear symptoms of the consequences: industrial wasteland, faded boulevards and economically depressed residential areas with social problems.

Nevertheless, money flows into the city. Chicago's commodity exchange for agricultural products is the most important one in the world. The city's airport is the world's largest. The Renaissance Center in Detroit represents a new beginning back in the '70s. From Lake Erie, the centre's glass towers extend skywards as a sort of proclamation to motivate the locals, 'We can do it!'

Moving away from the lake's banks beyond Chicago, the region is dominated by agriculture: wheat, corn, soy beans and seemingly endless pastures. Toward the north, the lakes become rougher. Even early in autumn, Lake Superior is marked by rough waves. This is not the only lake in the state of Minnesota, whose automobile license plates bear the title 'Land of 10,000 Lakes'. Water and forests, fishing villages and vacation resorts comprise the western edge of the Great Lakes: there you'll find scenery which has not been touched by industry, neither yesterday nor today.

CHICAGO

(102/A4) Chicago, with its population of 'only' eight million, has lost the honour of being the second-largest city in America to Los Angeles. But the metropolis on the southwest corner of Lake Michigan, an old city of slaughterhouses and gangsters, still feels like it's the 'No. 2 City'. Chicago aims to maintain its cultural and architectural image. Chicago boasts the oldest skyscraper in the world, the Monadnock Building built in 1891, and the former world's tallest building, the Sears Tower (442 m/1,436 ft). The Chicago Symphony Orchestra is perhaps one of the best in the world, and the city's museums can only be beaten by what New York has to offer. The architectural dynamics of the city are a result of the great fire from 1871, after which the city had to be completely rebuilt. The local, innovative architectural trend continued into the 20th century — with architects such as Louis Sullivan, Mies van der Rohe and Frank Lloyd Wright. Yet Chicago is not only a magnificent showcase of architecture, but also the pulsating economical heart of the Midwest — not to mention the northern centre for jazz, blues and modern art.

SIGHTS

The main street in Chicago is Michigan Avenue, which runs parallel to the shore of Lake Michigan. The downtown area is located south of the narrow Chicago River in and around the 'Loop' — an elevated railway line. This is where to find the most skyscrapers as well as postmodern structures: the State of Illinois Building by American star architect Helmut Jahn, the Civic Center with a 15-m (49-ft) tall Picasso sculpture, the Sears Tower and the Board of Trade Building. Shopping centres and large hotels are situated north of the river around Michigan Avenue. West of there are art galleries and ☂ the area around Rush Street, renowned for its great nightlife.

John Hancock Center

★ A city within the city: the 100-floor skyscraper houses office and living space. The observation platform provides a ☾ magnificent view of Lake Michigan and Lakeshore Drive. *Daily 9am-midnight; Admission: $3.65; 875 North Michigan Ave.*

Shedd Aquarium

Six thousand fish, sea lions and otters — and a grand ☾ view of the Chicago skyline. *Daily 9am-6pm; Admission: $11, 1200 South Lakeshore Dr.; Tel: (312) 939-2438*

MUSEUMS

Art Institute of Chicago

One of the best art museums in the world. *Mon-Fri 10:30am-4.30pm, Sat 10am-5pm, Sun 12-5pm; Admission: $6; South Michigan Ave./Adams St.; Tel: (312) 443-3600*

Chicago Architecture

Daily tours with varying themes on the architectural highlights of the city. Tours are either on foot, by coach or by boat. *Times vary, phone for information beforehand, price per tour starts at $10; 224 South Michigan Ave.; Tel: (312) 922-3432*

RESTAURANTS

The Butcher Shop

Steak, steak and more steak. *358 West Ontario St.; Tel: (312) 440-4900; Category 2*

Le Mikado

A memorable mixture of French and Chinese cuisine. Tastes excellent! *21 West Goethe St.; Tel: (312) 280-8611; Category 2*

The 95th

The place to come for a beautiful ❧ view of Chicago's city lights in the evening. Also serves a delicious Sunday brunch. *John Hancock Center, 875 North Michigan Ave.; Tel: (312) 787-9596; Category 2*

HOTELS

Essex Inn

High-quality service and inexpensive, on the southern edge of the city. *255 rooms; 800 South Michigan Ave.; Tel: (312) 939-2800; Fax: 939-1605; Category 2*

The Fairmont

Neoclassical architectural style with ❧ a charming view of the lake and Grant Park. *692 rooms; 200 North Columbus Dr.; Tel: (312) 565-8000; Fax: 856-1032; Category 1*

ENTERTAINMENT

Chicago's nightlife is excellent. Most clubs and bars are located within the Loop around Halstead and Rush Street on the North Side. For blues try the B.L.U.E.S (2519 North Halstead St.), for jazz the Bulls (1916 North Lincoln Park West) or the Green Mill (4802 North Broadway). Announcements of the scheduled performances are found in the *Chicago Reader* or in the Friday edition of the *Tribune.*

INFORMATION

Office of Tourism's Visitor Information Center

Chicago Cultural Center, 78 East Washington St.; Tel: (312) 744-2400

CINCINNATI

(102/C6) The largest city (pop. 1 million) of this midwestern state is located in southern Ohio between the hills on the northern banks of the Ohio River, which also forms the border to Kentucky. After its founding in 1788, Cincinnati rose to become an important trade and industrial city, providing a high quality of life, even today. The modern downtown area is situated around *Fountain Square* at the foot of the 48-storey ❧ *Carew Tower* (observation platform). Also worth seeing is the elegant business and residential area called *Mt. Adams* and several outstanding *art museums.* After 1830 Cincinnati was an important destination for German immigrants whose descendants continue to celebrate Oktoberfest each September in the traditional manner.

RESTAURANTS

Mike Fink
Good fish restaurant on an old river steamboat, magnificent ✦ view of the city's skyline. *Covington, Kentucky, at the foot of Greenup St.; Tel: (606) 261-4212; Category 2*

INFORMATION

Cincinnati Visitors' Bureau
300 West 6th St., Cincinnati, OH 45202; Tel: (513) 621-2142

CLEVELAND

(**103/D5**) This Ohio harbour city (pop. 2.7 million in the greater metropolitan area) on the southern bank of Lake Erie was one of the most important industrial areas at the turn of the last century. This is where John D. Rockefeller made his millions. Following the slow and painful downfall of the city, it has regained some of its former attractiveness in recent years: The *Waterfront* along the lake and the old warehouse areas have been restored, the *University Circle* district now houses some excellent museums and Christoph von Dohnányi led the *Cleveland Orchestra* to world prominence.

SIGHTS

Good-time III
Harbour boat rides from May to Sept.; Admission: $10; departure from North Coast Harbor; Tel: (216) 861-5110

COLUMBUS

(**102–103/C–D6**) The Ohio state capital (pop. 633,000) is the home of the famous Ohio State University, one of the most important centres of technology in America. The *museum of technology* 'COSI' and the *open-air museum* Ohio Village are definitely worth seeing.

DETROIT

(**102/C4**) Detroit is America's automobile capital. Henry Ford invented the assembly line here and this is where the great automobile factories of General Motors, Ford and Chrysler are located. The city on the Detroit River, which forms part of the border to Canada, remains the most important metropolis in Michigan. One million people live in Detroit. The metropolitan area totals 4.7 million. Strikes, uprisings and a high crime rate combined to give the city a bad reputation. The downtown area was pretty desolate 20 years ago, but over the past decade it has made a comeback. The heart of downtown now boasts the glass towers of the ✦ *Renaissance Center*. Areas such as *Greektown* and the *Theater District* have been restored and have become favourite places to take an evening stroll.

MUSEUMS

Henry Ford Museum
★ The history of the automobile industry and the role of the automobile in American society are the focal points of this huge museum complex. *Greenfield Village* is an adjoining open-air museum, containing historical buildings and Thomas Edison's laboratory. *Daily 9am-5pm; Admission: $12.50; museum and village $22, Dearborn; Tel: (313) 271-1620*

Motown Museum

The Motown recording studio for such stars as Smokey Robinson, Diana Ross and the Supremes was in this inconspicuous house from 1959 to 1972. *Tues-Sat 10am-5pm, Sun and Mon 12-5pm; Admission: $6; 2648 W Grand Blvd.; Tel: (313) 875-2264*

Westin Renaissance Center

An exclusive hotel with 1,400 luxurious rooms in a 230-m (748-ft) tall tower. *Hart Plaza; Tel: (313) 568-8000; Fax: 568-8146; Category 1*

HOTELS

Shorecrest Motor Inn

Simple motel; clean and near downtown. *54 rooms; 1316 E Jefferson Ave.; Tel: (313) 568-3000; Fax: 568-3002; Category 3*

INFORMATION

Detroit Visitor Information Center

2 E Jefferson Ave., Detroit, MI 48226; Tel: (313) 567-1170

Niagara Falls in upstate New York

INDIANAPOLIS

(**102/B6**) The Indiana state capital is also the largest city in this midwestern state (pop. 1.2 million). The claim to fame for Indianapolis, located in the middle of the state, is the *Indianapolis 500.* This legendary automobile race over 500 miles has been conducted on the last Sunday in May since 1911. The speedway, north of the city, attracts 500,000 spectators, making it America's largest sports event. Automobile fans should visit the *Hall of Fame Museum* — open year-round — which features the Speedway's famous race car drivers. The modern downtown area features the *Eiteljorg Museum of American Indian and Western Art* which is worth a visit.

MILWAUKEE

(**102/A3**) Milwaukee (pop. 1.6 million) on the west bank of Lake Michigan was once a very German city — and is the capital of breweries. Although German ceased being the dominant language here after World War I and the breweries do not conform with German brewer's specifications, Milwaukee has still managed to maintain a Teutonic flair with quiet residential streets and numerous German restaurants. A visit to the breweries is worthwhile (*guided tours at Pabst and Miller*).

NIAGARA FALLS

(**103/F3**) The famous waterfalls along the Niagara River between Lake Erie and Lake Ontario have two nationalities: American and Canadian. While the water on the American side falls further — 56 m (182 ft) — the falls on the Canadian side are more impressive; the depth is two metres less: 54 m (175 ft), but the expanse is much wider — 670 m (2198 ft). From ★ *Goat Island,* a small island that separates the two waterfalls, you'll have a fantastic ☙ view of the adjacent falls.

TOURS

Maid of the Mist
You can approach the foot of the thundering waterfall in a small boat. Raincoats are provided by the tour guides. *Every half hour, daily 10am-6pm; Admission: $8; departure at the base of the Observation Tower on Prospect Point; Tel: (716) 284-4233*

SAULT STE. MARIE

(**102/C3**) The main attraction of this small city in the forested area of northern Michigan are the huge locks on St. Mary's River, the waterway connecting Lake Superior with Lake Huron. The parks on both sides of the river provide a good ☙ view of the locks and the continual traffic of freight ships.

SURROUNDING AREA

Mackinac Island (**102/C2-3**)
★ An hour's drive south of Sault Ste. Marie, a 6-km (4-mile) long suspension bridge connects the straits between Lake Michigan and Lake Huron. At the south end you'll find the historical little town of *Mackinaw City,* where ferries depart for *Mackinac Island* where the historic *Fort Mackinac* (museum) is located.

Exploring America

*These routes are marked in green on the map inside front flap
and in the road atlas beginning on page 100*

① THE SOUTH: AZALEAS AND CHERRY BLOSSOMS

 This spring tour leads from the capital of Washington, D.C., to the haert of the South: Virginia, North and South Carolina and Georgia. The southern-most point of the route is Tallahas-see, the capital of Florida. On the way down South via Charleston and Savannah, a slight detour will lead you over the Outer Banks, while the return trip will take you through the Appalachians. The tour is about 4,000 km (2,500 miles) long and takes about 14 days. The cherry blossoms at the end of April signify the arrival of spring. The romantic southern states are quickly flooded by a sea of blossoms. The humid heat of the summer is still far away, enabling you to enjoy the magnificent mansions of another era. And you can save a visit to the beach or a hike through the mountains for the sunniest days – a welcome reprise from the museums and mansions.

Washington, D.C. (p. 51) is easy to reach from any airport in the USA, Canada or Europe via its two international airports, Washington Dulles and Baltimore Washington International. If you're leaving from New York, the best destination is the centrally located aiport for domestic flights, recently renamed the Ronald Reagan National. The cherry trees surrounding the *Jefferson Monument* are in full bloom at the end of April. The trees were a present from the Japanese. At this time of year, it's easy to walk down the impressive *Mall,* the promenade between the monuments and the Capitol, with its series of *museums.* A brief stay in this city allows travellers from abroad to become accustomed to the time difference. The neoclassical style of the government buildings and countless museums provides the pomp and circumstance expected of a world power. But the columns and style of the *White House,* set apart geographically from the strip of government buildings, are the first introduction to the architectural style of the South. And the residential areas of the *Northwest* district remind visitors that, until it became the nation's capital, Washington wasn't much more than a small southern town. The early colonial style is most evident in the enchanting suburbs of *George-town,* where Secretary of State Madelaine Albright's villa is located, and in *Alexandria* on the other side of the Potomac River. A pure form of colonial beginnings can be seen in *Williamsburg (p. 63)*, the museum town in southeastern Virginia. Horse-drawn carriages roll down the streets in this 'living museum', craftsmen perform their trades and crops are planted as in the olden days. Actors talk with visitors in the taverns — so you feel like you've been propelled back to the 18th century!

Leaving Williamsburg, it's not too far until you reach the islands off the coast of North Carolina, the *Outer Banks (p. 61)*. The islands are connected to the mainland by bridges and ferries and feature a scenery of high sand dunes. The Atlantic is relatively quiet here in the springtime yet still a bit cool to stay in the water for too long. The hurricanes don't come until late summer. The notorious *Bermuda Triangle* is located in the ocean just off the islands. Boats and airplanes have repeatedly disappeared mysteriously over this area. The real explanation for this phenomenon is more likely to be the combination of the Gulf Stream and extremely strong storms. The raw forces of nature can be seen in the continually changing path of the beach. Some buildings and streets have even disappeared along these shorelines. But mankind and nature often join forces, and not only in negative ways: the Wright brothers completed their first successful attempts at flying, up on the tall sand dunes.

Back on the mainland, the route continues along the coast in a southwest direction. You can easily avoid the beach resort which is really a huge amusement park, *Myrtle Beach*, by taking a side route. The goal of this stretch of the journey is *Charleston (p. 59)*.

If you leave on a morning ferry from *Ocracoke (p. 62)* on the Outer Banks to *Cedar Island* you can still reach Charleston by evening. There the glory of the great *Antebellum mansions awaits you*, the time before the American Civil War which was fought from 1860 to 1865. The azaleas, the symbol of southern vegetation, are in full bloom. Charleston isn't too far away from *Savannah (p. 62)*, just on the other side of the border between South Carolina and Georgia. The Spanish moss suspended from the oak trees gives the first city to have been completely planned in a grid pattern a somewhat dark flair, yet with the increasing heat you're thankful for every bit of shade.

The next stretch of the journey takes you via *Waycross* and *Valdosta* to *Tallahassee*. None of the places along the way are worth staying at long. But in this part of the South, which has not been groomed for tourists, you notice traces of the old charm as well as the old poverty. Except for the cars, you begin to feel yourself taking a step back in time to Antebellum.

Atlanta (p. 56) provides the absolute contrast to the old South. It is the symbol of the new, booming and increasingly industrialized South. Don't expect a beautiful city, but an interesting one. The residential area of *Buckhead* is the only truly beautiful area. In contrast, the downtown area is something of a city of the future for hot climates, which is unthinkable without the omnipresent air-conditioning and the covered atriums.

When you're making the return trip — the main route is on

Interstate 85 — then you can take a detour toward the west into the Appalachians and hike on part of the *Appalachian Trail*. The *Great Smoky Mountains* in North Carolina and the *Skyline Drive* in Virginia are especially beautiful. *Charlottesville (p. 61)* is the last worthwhile stop on this route. The main sight to see is the *University of Virginia,* built by Thomas Jefferson, which boasts the most harmonious campus in the world.

② NEW ENGLAND: MELTING POT AND AUTUMN LEAVES

 The best time to take this tour is in summer or autumn. It starts in New York City and continues through the Yankee states: Connecticut, Massachusetts, New Hampshire, Maine, Vermont and New York state. The northernmost point is Acadia National Park in Maine. On the return trip, it's possible to take a detour to Niagara Falls, but you'll have to plan an extra two days of travel time. If you make the trip in the summertime, it's better to save New York City for the end of the journey because it can be unbearably hot in the city of skyscrapers. And there are also fewer cultural events in the Big Apple then. The route is about 1,800 km (1,125 miles) long, or 2,800 km (1,750 miles) long including Niagara Falls, and takes ten to 14 days. When Indian summer, the most beautiful time of year, begins, you can still spend time in other places besides the beach or at a mountain lake. Although the leaves on the trees change colour, it can even still be quite warm in mid-October. You won't want to miss Boston, the city of American patriots, and Cape Cod, the favourite beach of the established intellectual and financial elite. Further north, you'll be fascinated by the raw charm of the rocky coast of Maine and the mountains of New Hampshire and Vermont – the solitude there is surprising. After that quiet atmosphere, your nerves will be ready for New York – the city that never sleeps.

If you have decided to save visiting the Big Apple until the end of your trip, then it's best to rent a car upon arriving at one of the major New York airports, for example, John F. Kennedy or Newark in New Jersey. Once in your car, depart toward Connecticut on Interstate 95 (from JFK take the Van Wyck Expressway, Interstate 678 North, then from Newark directly onto Interstate 95 which is called the New Jersey Turnpike).

The first stop in Connecticut is the *Mystic Seaport (p. 44)* beyond *New London*. The *open-air museum* shows what life was like in a typical harbour town in the New World. From there you drive via *Providence* in the small state of Rhode Island toward Cape Cod, the next destination. If you'd like to take a dip in the ocean while on Rhode Island, then take the coastal route US 1 instead of staying on Interstate 95. *Cape Cod (p. 42)*, the hook-shaped peninsula, is longer than you'd expect. We recommend simply selecting a place to stay according to what appeals to you the most in one of the towns on Cape Cod, such as *Hyannis* or *Provincetown (p. 42)* or somewhere in between. But if you'll be there over the Labor Day weekend (the weekend before the first Monday in September), make sure you reserve a hotel ahead of time. That weekend signifies the end of the summer season. Following Labor Day, it's easy to find accommodation. The clam chowder, a soup of mussels, and the lobster served here are reason enough for the fish and seafood connoisseur to make the journey. Restaurants are on every street corner and most of them serve good food. The beaches are extremely long and, despite the great popularity of Cape Cod, are not as full as European beaches.

By now you've had enough rest and relaxation to gather strength for the next major city. *Boston (p. 40)* is about four hours from Provincetown. The veritable capital of Massachusetts, where the settlers basically declared what became known as the Revolutionary War on the British Crown with their famous *Boston Tea Party* , can easily be explored on foot. The same applies to the campus of *Harvard University* and nearby *Cambridge (p. 42)*.

After Boston the route continues on Interstate 95. Outside *Brunswick* in Maine you turn onto US 1 and continue along the rocky coast toward the climax of the journey, *Acadia National Park (p. 39)*. The bright-coloured boats of the lobster fishermen bob on the water in the small, rocky bays. This is where shellfish is caught, and where lobster is eaten like sausage in other parts of the world. Look for a well-situated Bed & Breakfast in the enchanting little towns. That's the best place to imbibe the atmosphere. Soon, you'll feel like part of this place, like a lobster fisherman himself!

Heading westward to New Hampshire, straight for *Berlin.* The *White Mountain National Forest* is used primarily by winter sports enthusiasts. But it's also an ideal place for hiking in the summer and autumn. We recommend taking a slight detour from the main route; the same applies to the neighbouring state of Vermont. Drive for a while on the New Hampshire side of the Connecticut River and then perhaps take a detour to Lake Chamberlain in Vermont where you start to get a feel for the expanse of the forest and lake countryside just across the border in Canada.

The *Niagara Falls (p. 87)* are truly breathtaking and romantic. Even the most wonderful Marilyn Monroe movie cannot communicate the feeling of truly being there. But you must take into account that trip from *Burlington* in Vermont to Niagara Falls takes an entire day just to get there *(US 7, US 4, Interstate 87, Interstate 90).*

Now it's time to return to New York City, where the best thing to do is to return your car as quickly as possible, because the city of all cities is best explored using the subway, taxi or on foot.

You've seen enough of nature, so now it's time to see the sights of the Big Apple — the skyscrapers, the museums, the shopping and a nightlife that never ends. Don't forget to take a short break in the public gardens of *Trump Tower*, one of the few places in the world where the average person can catch a glimpse of what it would be like to own a penthouse.

Practical information

Here you'll find important addresses and other useful information for your trip in the eastern USA

AMERICAN ENGLISH

In North America, certain terms and usages deviate from British usage. Some of the more frequently encountered examples are: *gas* for *petrol*, *trunk* for *boot*, *car rental* for *car hire*, *toll-free numbers* for *freephone numbers*, *wait staff* for *waiting staff* (in restaurants etc.). In case of doubt you should consult a dictionary.

BUSINESS HOURS

Stores are primarily open daily from 9am to 9pm. Large malls Mon–Sat from 10 am to 9 pm and Sun from 12pm to 5pm. Large drugstores and supermarkets are also open in the evenings and on weekends, some even 24 hours a day. Museums are usually open from 9am to 5pm and Sun from 1pm to 5pm, and often closed on Mon.

CAMPING

The public campgrounds are generally the most beautiful: they are located in the midst of nature along lakes and in National Parks they are equipped with the basics (grill, picnic tables, shower facilities). An overnight stay costs between \$5 and \$15. On the outskirts of cities and parks, you'll find privately run, relatively luxuriously equipped campgrounds with hot showers, a swimming pool and stores (prices range from \$10 to \$30). We recommend the KOA chain, one of the largest in the country, which also takes reservations. Except for in the parks, it's not prohibited to camp anywhere, although it is frowned upon in well-populated areas.

You can also rent a camper or RV (recreational vehicle), but it's best to reserve months ahead of your trip.

CAR RENTAL

All you need in order to rent a car is your driver's licence. Smaller companies sometimes require an international driver's licence. Rental cars are especially inexpensive, starting at approx. \$25 per day and \$120 per week, and unlimited mileage is nearly always included in the rental agreement.

A loss/damage waiver costs an additional \$10 to \$13 per day. Please note: even if this extra insurance is already paid per voucher, or covered through payment with a credit card, the rental agents sometimes try to add the cost for the insurance to the bill. Minimum age to rent a car: 21, sometimes 25 years. In addition to the large rental companies such as Alamo, Avis, Budget and Hertz, regional companies are frequently less expensive, making them a good alternative for city visits. However, they are not worthwhile for an extended tour. It is cheaper and safer to reserve a car in advance and return it in the same city.

CUSTOMS

Plants, meat, fruit and other fresh grocery items may not be brought into the country in order to prevent the spread of animal and plant diseases.

Adults are allowed to import 200 cigarettes or 50 cigars (no Cuban brands) and 1 litre of liquor plus gifts worth a total of $100.

DOMESTIC FLIGHTS

American airlines offer quite a number of inexpensive flights, if you can find your way through the jungle of prices. Please note that a wide variety of conditions apply: booking ahead, length of stay or if a weekend is included. Flights booked on short notice are as expensive as in Europe.

DRIVING

The infrastructure of the road system is excellent. The motorways are classified according to numbers for better orientation. Each type of roadway has a differ-

ent kind of sign: county roads, state and U.S. routes, as well as the wide interstates. Seat belts must be fastened, according to law. The speed limit on state routes is generally 55 mph (88 km/h), and within city limits 35 mph (50 km/h). The speed limit on the interstates ranges from 65-75 mph (105-120 km/h).

It is permissable to turn right at a red light, as long as there is no sign saying 'No turn on red'. It is also possible to pass cars on the right-hand side on the motorways. School buses with red blinking lights and a displayed stop sign, may not be passed – from either direction. When approaching 4-way stop signs, or any intersections where each direction has a stop sign, the vehicle that arrives and stops at the intersection first, is allowed to continue first.

The *American Automobile Association* (AAA – called Triple A) also provides assistance to members of automobile clubs in other countries, so don't forget your membership card!

EMBASSIES & CONSULATES

Canadian Embassy
501 Pennsylvania Ave. NW, Washington, D.C.; Tel: (202) 682-1755

Canadian Consulates
in the following cities:
Atlanta: *400 South Tower, CNN Center, Atlanta, GA 30303-2705; Tel: (404) 577-6810*
Boston: *Suite 400, Copley Place, Boston, MA 02116; Tel: (617) 262-3760*
Detroit: *Suite 1100, 600 Renaissance Center, Detroit, MI 48243-1704; Tel: (313) 567-2340*
New York: *16th Floor, Exxon*

Building, 1251 Avenue of the Americas, New York, NY 10020-1175; Tel: (212) 745-0200

British Embassy
3100 Massachusetts Ave. NW, Washington, D.C. 20008; Tel: (202) 462-1340

British Consulate
845 Third Avenue, New York NY 10022; Tel: (212) 745-0200

In case of an emergency, dial '911'. This number applies nearly everywhere in the USA and can be dialed for free from every telephone. In rural areas, a different number may apply for the police, fire department or ambulance. If you can't find a number, dial '0' for the operator.

Medical facilities in the USA are very good, but expensive. Non-American travellers should take out the appropriate medical coverage for their trip. Medical prescriptions can be filled at *pharmacies* or *drugstores*.

General information: The *USTTA (United States Travel and Tourism Administration)* has offices located throughout the world, generally in American embassies and consulates. Great Britain *Tel: (0171) 495-4466; Mon-Fri, 10am-4pm* .

American Society of Travel Agents (ASTA) *Tel: (800) 965-2782 (24-hour hotline, toll-free when calling within the U.S.)*

Alliance of Canadian Travel Association, *1729 Bank Street, Suite 201, Ottawa, Ontario K1V 7Z5, Canada; Tel: (613) 521-0474*

Association of British Travel Agents *55-57 Newman Street, London W1P 4AH, England; Tel: (0171) 637-244*

Travel and Tourism Offices (all 1-800 telephone numbers are for dialling within the USA)

The smallest post office in the world in Ochopee, Florida

Connecticut	(800) 282-6863
Delaware	(800) 441-8846
District of	
Columbia	(202) 789-7000
Florida	(904) 487-1462
Georgia	(800) 847-4842
Kentucky	(800) 225-8747
Maryland	(800) 543-1036
Massachusetts	(800) 447-6277
Michigan	(800) 543-2937
Minnesota	(800) 657-3700
Mississippi	(800) 927-6378
Missouri	(800) 877-1234
New Hampshire	(800) 386-4664
New Jersey	(800) 537-7397
New York	(800) 225-5697
North Carolina	(800) 847-4862
Ohio	(800) 282-5393
Pennsylvania	(800) 847-4872
Rhode Island	(800) 556-2484
South Carolina	(800) 346-3634
Tennessee	(800) 836-6200
Vermont	(800) 837-6668

MONEY

Banks are generally open from 9am to 3pm (Fri until 5.30 pm). You can cash traveller's cheques which have been issued in US dollars, but only larger banks exchange foreign currency. It is possible to change European currencies for US dollars in large cities, at international airports and in some of the major hotels, but the exchange rate is usually not as good.

It's better to take dollars on your travels, and to divide money into various categories: about *$100 cash* for your arrival, *traveller's cheques* in dollars (accepted in most restaurants and stores, and you receive the change in cash) for daily expenditures, credit cards for larger expenses and emergencies (Visa and Eurocard are accepted more frequently than American Express). Credit cards are accepted almost everywhere. Eurocheques are not accepted. For non-North American travellers: the currency is the American dollar (= *100 cents*). Bank notes are available in 1, 2, 5, 10, 20, 50 and 100 dollar *bills* and *coins* in 1 ¢ *(penny)*, 5 ¢ *(nickel)*, 10 ¢ *(dime)*, 25 ¢ *(quarter)* and 50 ¢ *(half dollar)*.

PASSPORTS & VISAS

Canadian citizens need only to present their birth certificate. For longer stays, it's better to take a passport. Canadians do not require a visa, even if their visit exceeds three months. British citizens who are staying less than 90 days also do not require a visa prior to entering the United States. However, every non-US resident must fill out an entry form upon entry, whether one arrives by airplane or across North American borders, which is checked by the customs officials.

PUBLIC TRANSPORT

All major metropolitan cities and many smaller communities can be reached by both of the coach companies Greyhound and Peter Pan Trailways. For detailed information on the routes and prices, call 1-800-231-2222 (from within the USA). Special passes are available for non-American travellers but must be purchased in your home country before commencing your journey. Inquire at a local travel agency.

RAILWAY

The railway network in the U.S. is not as extensive as in Europe and only useful for a large tour.

The passenger railway company Amtrak offers a 'USA Eastern Pass' for unlimited travel in the eastern USA. Information is available by ringing Tel: (800) USA-RAIL or (800) 872-7245. Internet: http://www.amtrak.com.

SALES TAX

Most states collect 4 to 7 per cent tax on all items sold. This *sales tax* is not calculated until the goods are totalled at the cash register, so please note that the price listed on products or on a menu does not include the tax. Additional tax ranging from 10 to 15 per cent is collected on hotel accommodation.

TELEPHONE

All telephone numbers in the USA have seven digits. Long-distance calls include a three-digit prefix known as the *area code*. For local calls, simply dial the seven-digit number. For long distance calls, dial '1', the area code and then the number.

Local calls from a telephone box cost 25 to 35¢. A computerized operator will announce the charge after a long-distance number is dialed. Please note: hotels often add high service charges. You'll save money by using a credit card, by first dialling the toll-free number of the telephone company, such as AT&T: 1-800-CALL ATT.

For assistance when making a telephone call, just dial '0' for the operator who can also connect collect calls.

The prefix when calling from the UK to the USA is 001. The prefix when calling from Canada

or the USA to Great Britain is: 011-44. Another bit of useful information for non-North American travellers: the toll-free numbers with the prefix '800' or '888' can be used to book flights, hotel accommodation and rental cars.

TIME ZONES

New England, East Coast, Florida: *Eastern Time Zone* (GMT - 5 hours); Mississippi Valley and west of Chicago: *Central Time Zone* (GMT - 6 hours). Please note: daylight savings time (+1 hour) begins the first Sunday in April and lasts until the last Sunday in October!

TIPPING

Service is not included in prices listed on a menu in restaurants. Thus, it is customary to leave 15% of the total bill on the table as a tip. Some restaurants automatically add this amount to the bill.

VOLTAGE

110 Volt, 60 Hertz. Plugs differ from those in European countries so you should purchase an adapter before commencing your journey. Some hair dryers and electric razors can switch from 110 to 220 volts.

WHEN TO GO

If you consider the sheer size of the United States, the differences in climate can be compared to the climatic range from North Africa to Sweden. Summer is the best time of year to travel in the northern states – the only disadvantage is that it's in the middle of the summer holidays. Spring and autumn are the best times of year to travel to the southern states, which can be unbelievably humid in the summer. And the best time to visit southern Florida is winter. The winters in the Midwest and New England are usually much colder than in Europe.

YOUTH HOSTELS

American Youth Hostels (AYH) cost between $3 and $25 per night.

The AYH network does not include nearly as many hostels as in Europe, but you'll generally find one in many of the larger cities and in some of the National Parks. A listing of the youth hostels is available in bookstores or at any national association of youth hostels: *Hostelling International, Vol. 2.* Another inexpensive alternative for accommodation is the *YMCA* (for men) and the *YWCA* (for women), although not every facility provides overnight accommodation.

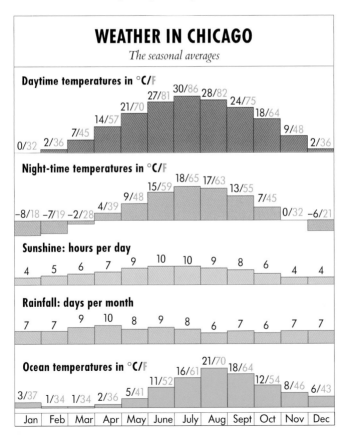

WEATHER IN CHICAGO

The seasonal averages

Daytime temperatures in °C/F

Jan	Feb	Mar	Apr	May	June	July	Aug	Sept	Oct	Nov	Dec
0/32	2/36	7/45	14/57	21/70	27/81	30/86	28/82	24/75	18/64	9/48	2/36

Night-time temperatures in °C/F

Jan	Feb	Mar	Apr	May	June	July	Aug	Sept	Oct	Nov	Dec
-8/18	-7/19	-2/28	4/39	9/48	15/59	18/65	17/63	13/55	7/45	0/32	-6/21

Sunshine: hours per day

Jan	Feb	Mar	Apr	May	June	July	Aug	Sept	Oct	Nov	Dec
4	5	6	7	9	10	10	9	8	6	4	4

Rainfall: days per month

Jan	Feb	Mar	Apr	May	June	July	Aug	Sept	Oct	Nov	Dec
7	7	9	10	8	9	8	6	7	6	7	7

Ocean temperatures in °C/F

Jan	Feb	Mar	Apr	May	June	July	Aug	Sept	Oct	Nov	Dec
3/37	1/34	1/34	2/36	5/41	11/52	16/61	21/70	18/64	12/54	8/46	6/43

Do's and don'ts

How to avoid some of the pitfalls
that face the unwary traveller

Accepting all invitations

Owing to the general friendliness and politeness of Americans, you'll often hear, 'If you're ever in Boston (or wherever the person lives), we'll have to get together!' – This, however, does not necessarily mean you really should take the person up on his offer, even if you exchange telephone numbers and addresses. An invitation is truly made when you agree on a date and time to meet. Otherwise, it is better to simply thank the person for his offer and add this conversation to one of the nice memories of your trip.

Shaking hands

Hi, how are you? Nice to meet you. This is what someone says after being introduced to you. If you reach out your hand in a friendly gesture you might find it dangling uncomfortably in the air. In America, shaking hands is something for politicians, businessmen and old friends. People who hardly know each other don't shake hands. It's sufficient to say your (first) name and to add 'I'm doing fine' or 'My pleasure'.

Parks after dark

As tempting as America's parks may be, it's a good idea to avoid them after sundown, as the crime rate, especially in the large cities, is still increasing. Youth involved in gangs are contributing to these statistics, as well as the ease at which firearms can be purchased.

Ignoring 'No Parking' signs

No parking means just that. And the police happily oblige in having your car towed. Because it's a fantastic way to fill up the empty treasuries of the local communities. Expect to pay $75 or more – in cash – plus a penalty.

Revving it up

You're waiting at a red light, and the person in the car next to you lets his engine roar, revving it up – an invitation to partake in a small race once the light turns green. Let him race onward, but without you. He has a souped-up motor, you don't. He'll just keep racing away from the police. They'll stop you instead.

Being mugged

Your money or your life! That's the threat during many robberies, even today. If it ever happens to you, do not resist in any way! Whoever is threatening you is likely to apply any kind of violence necessary. The best thing to do is to surrender your money, which will probably save you from anything worse.

Road Atlas of the Eastern US

Please refer to the back cover for an overview of this road atlas

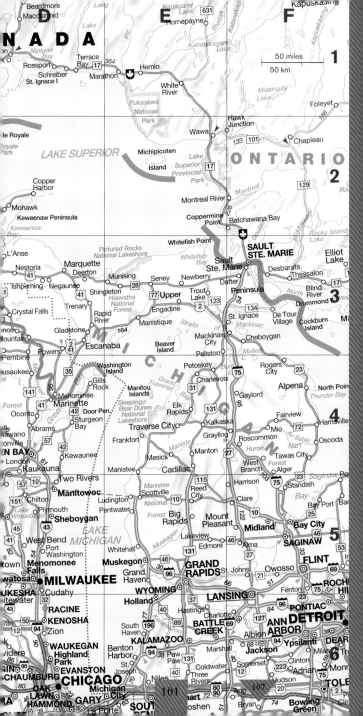

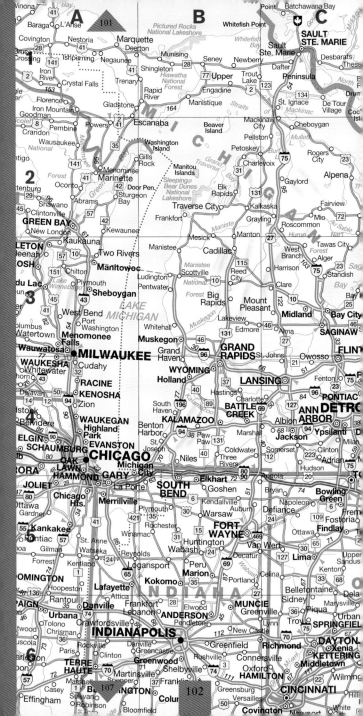

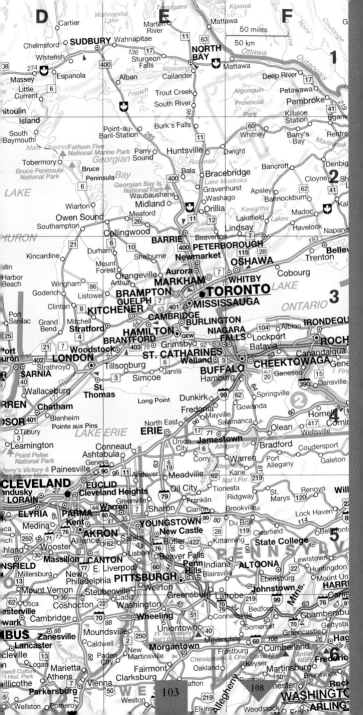

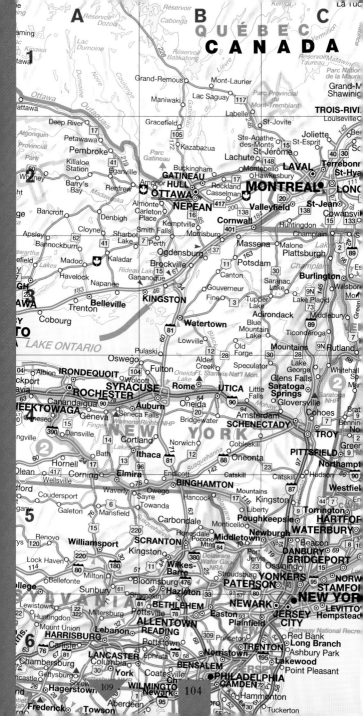

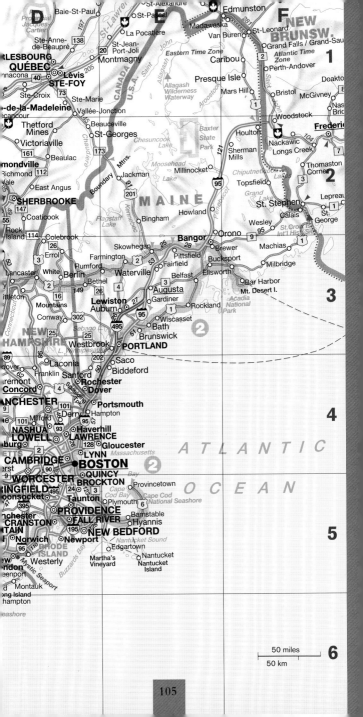

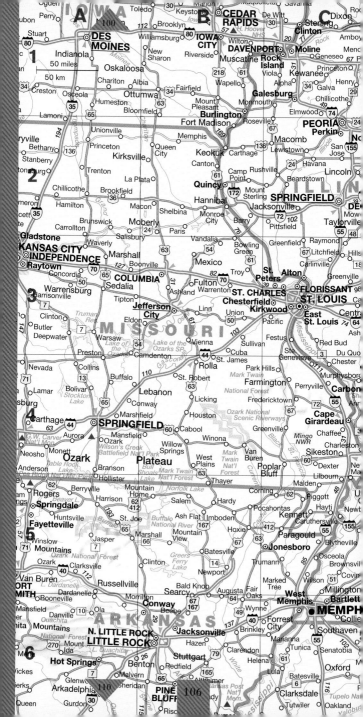

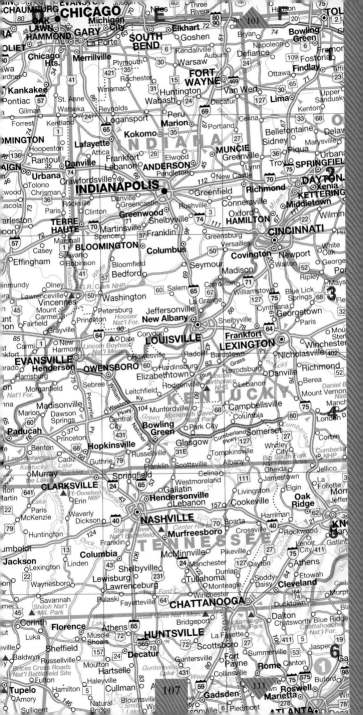

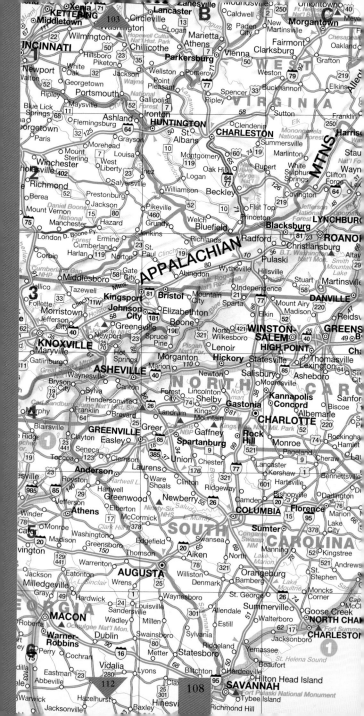

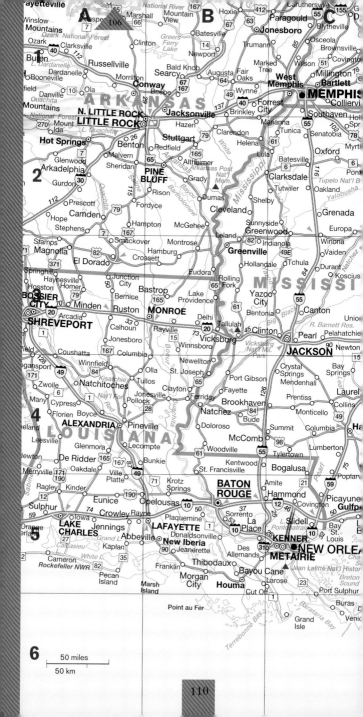

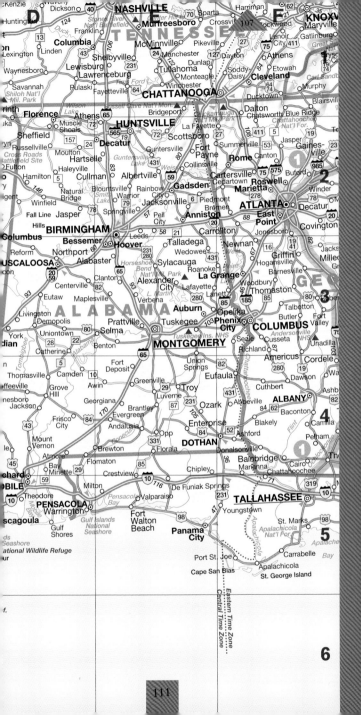

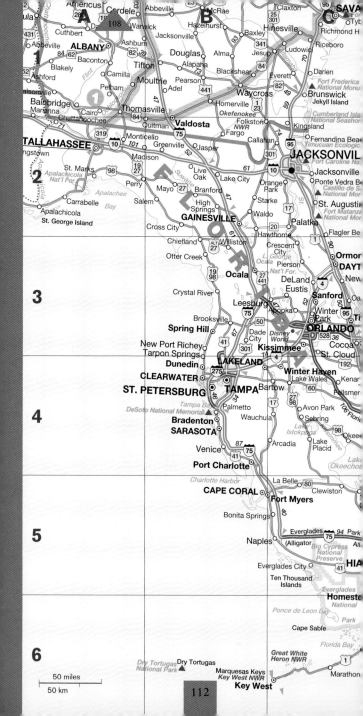

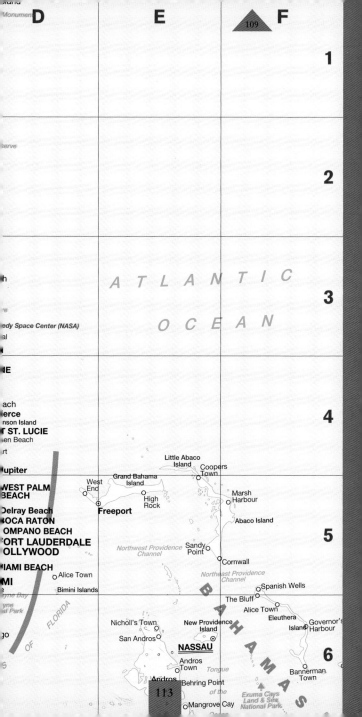

Monument

Monument

serve

h

re

edy Space Center (NASA)
al

IE

ach
ierce
nson Island
T ST. LUCIE
sen Beach
rt

Jupiter

**WEST PALM
BEACH**

**Delray Beach
BOCA RATON
OMPANO BEACH
ORT LAUDERDALE
OLLYWOOD**

IAMI BEACH
MI

yne Bay
al Park

go

s

ATLANTIC

OCEAN

FLORIDA

OF

Alice Town

Bimini Islands

Little Abaco
Island

Coopers
Town

West
End

Grand Bahama
Island

High
Rock

Freeport

Marsh
Harbour

Abaco Island

*Northwest Providence
Channel*

Sandy
Point

Cornwall

*Northeast Providence
Channel*

Spanish Wells

The Bluff

Alice Town

Eleuthera
Island

Governor's
Harbour

Nicholl's Town

New Providence
Island

San Andros

NASSAU

Andros
Town

Behring Point

*Tongue
of the*

Bannerman
Town

*Exuma Cays
Land & Sea
National Park*

Andros

Mangrove Cay

B A H A M A S

113

ROAD ATLAS LEGEND

Gebührenfreie Autobahn	═══════	Controlled access highway
Gebührenpflichtige Autobahn	═══════	Controlled access toll highway
Hauptverbindungsstraße	───────	Principal through highway
Nebenstraße	───────	Other through highway
Interstate highway	(20)	Interstate highway
US Highway	(98) (68)	US Highway
Trans-Kanada-Highway / Mexican Federal Highway	🍁 (14)	Trans-Canada Highway / Mexican Federal Highway
Bundesstaat-oder Provinzhighway	40 75	State or provincial highway
Entfernung (Meilen/Kilometer)	25 40	Distance (Miles/Kilometres)
Internationale Grenze	═══════	International boundary
Provinz- oder Bundesstaatengrenze	═══════	Provincial, territorial or state boundary
Fähre	─ ─ ─ ─ ─	Ferry
Zeitzonengrenze	....	Time zone boundary
National-, Bundesstaat- oder Provinzpark	═══════	National/State/Provincial Park
Erholungs- oder Schutzgebiet	═══════	Recreational area or reserve
Natursehenswürdigkeit	⛰	Natural point of interest
Kulturelle Sehenswürdigkeit	▲	Cultural point of interest

Einwohnerzahl:		Population:
Harrison	o	unter/less than 10 000
Camden	o	10 000 - 25 000
Muskegon	⊙	25 000 - 50 000
LONGVIEW	⊙	50 000 - 100 000
ALLENTOWN	◎	100 000 - 200 000
LONG BEACH	◉	200 000 - 500 000
MILWAUKEE	●	500 000 - 1 000 000
NEW YORK	●	über/more than 1 000 000
WASHINGTON		Hauptstadt / National capital
RICHMOND		Bundesstaats-/Provinzhauptstadt / State/Provinvcial/Territorial capital
Stadtgebiet		Built-up area

```
|———————————— 100 miles ————————————|
    |———————————— 100 km ————————————|
```

INDEX

This index lists all the main sights, attractions (e.g. National Parks, open-air museums, amusement parks) and hotels. Numbers in boldface refer to main entries, italics to photographs

Places

Attractions

Hotels

What do you get for your money?

Despite fluctuations in the exchange rate, the US dollar has remained relatively stable. In travelling there, you do not run the financial risk of losing money when exchanging dollars for your home currency at the end of your trip. Extremely low flight prices are another advantage of travelling to the USA. Airlines have been waging price wars to increase their market share of the trans-Atlantic flight business. This has kept prices for flights to the USA relatively low. Inflation has also slowed somewhat, keeping prices relatively stable. A ride with public transportation in US cities costs about $1.50. Taxi rides are generally reasonable. While coffee usually costs $2, sandwiches or hot dogs run $3. Mixed drinks cost around $5. Eating in restaurants is relatively inexpensive. It's possible to eat your fill for around $15 at most Chinese restaurants. Motel rooms, which are generally more comfortable than pensions in Europe, cost $60–$80 outside of large cities. The advantage: The price is the same no matter how many people stay in the room.

You'll feel like an outcast to the human race if you don't present a credit card. Paying in cash is very unusual. And don't forget: Eurocheques are not accepted in America!

US$	UK £	Can$
1	0.59	1.55
2	1.18	3.10
3	1.77	4.65
4	2.36	6.20
5	2.95	7.75
10	5.90	15.50
20	11.80	31.00
30	17.70	46.50
40	23.60	62.00
50	29.50	77.50
60	35.40	93.00
70	41.30	108.50
80	47.20	124.00
90	53.10	139.50
100	59.00	155.00
200	118.00	310.00
300	177.00	465.00
400	236.00	620.00
500	295.00	775.00
750	442.50	1162.50
1000	590.00	1550.00